HEART ON MY SLEEVE

Attila The Stockbroker

First published in Great Britain, September 2020 by Cherry Red Books (a division of Cherry Red Records), Power Road Studios, 114 Power Road, London W4 5PY.

© Attila The Stockbroker / John Baine 2020

ISBN: 978-1-909454-87-3

The author asserts the moral right to be identified as the author of this work. All rights reserved. No part of this book may be reproduced or transmitted in any form or by any means, electronic or manual, including photocopying, recording or any data retrieval system without written permission from the publisher. This book is sold subject to the condition that it shall not, by way of trade or otherwise, be lent, resold, hired out or otherwise circulated without the publisher's written consent in any form of binding or cover other than that in which it is published.

Cover design and book layout by Alan Wares

Front cover photograph by Robina Baine

Back cover photographs by Contingent, Tony Mottram, anon and Richard Nixon

Photograph on page 5 by Pat Blann; page 14 by Tony Mottram

Printed by Ashford Colour Press

To contact Attila for prospective gigs, interviews etc
Email: attila@attilathestockbroker.com
Facebook: facebook.com/attilathestockbroker
Twitter @atilatstokbroka
For books, CDs, T shirts etc, web: attilathestockbroker.bandcamp.com

HEART ON MY SLEEVE
COLLECTED WORKS 1980-2020

Attila The Stockbroker

With illustrations by

Phill 'Porky the Poet' Jupitus    *Womble*    *Dan Woods* 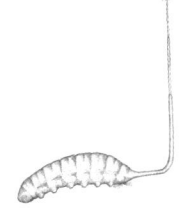   *Nick Staples*

CHERRY RED BOOKS

TO MY WIFE ROBINA IN LOCKDOWN, 8TH SEPTEMBER 2020

For forty years today I've lived this life:
Travelled the world for concerts far and wide.
For half of this, my love, you've been my wife:
A glorious inspiration at my side.
A quarter of each year or more apart.
For me a time to rant, for you to rest.
Then I return to you, my loving heart,
Resume our path together, two abreast.

When lockdown hit, at first I was bereft -
Though I believed it should have come before.
My travelling ways through all the years were gone.
The gigs I built my life around no more.
I thought, then wrote, then learned to broadcast live
Though IT still remains a fickle friend
My office now my gateway to my world –
A world I first feared would come to an end.

But now we were together all the time!
Strong characters, both set a brand new test.
My table manners and the toothpaste top.
This tireless tongue which never seems to rest.
But all our days were full of love and fun.
We never thought 'Something will have to give'.
We looked into each other's eyes and said
'No-one I'd rather be in lockdown with!'

I loved to watch our garden as it grew.
Not sometimes, this year: every single day.
Tomatoes from the seed to bright red fruit
Green beans to freezer from the starting tray.
Once lockdown eased a bit and summer came
My childhood years returned: my rods, my bike.
A few hours to ourselves now all we need.
A night apart now something not to like.

Heart On My Sleeve

One day, I hope, I'll hit the road again.
One day your peace and quiet will return.
But this great revelation in our love,
Enforced by fate, was wonderful to learn.
So, darling, thanks for marrying me full time.
A stroppy poet, loud of mouth and arse.
And as my valediction in this rhyme
I hereby dub you Comrade Wife, First Class.

BIBLIOGRAPHY & DISCOGRAPHY

POETRY BOOKS
1986   Cautionary Tales for Dead Commuters (Unwin)
1986   The Rising Sons of Ranting Verse with Seething Wells (Unwin)
1992   Scornflakes (Bloodaxe)
1998   The Rat-Tailed Maggot and Other Poems (Roundhead Publications)
2001   Goldstone Ghosts (Roundhead Publications)
2008   My Poetic Licence (Roundhead Publications)
2010   The Long Goodbye (Roundhead Publications)
2014   UK Gin Dependence Party and Other Peculiarities (Roundhead Publications)
2017   Undaunted (Roundhead Publications)
2020   Heart On My Sleeve (Cherry Red Books)

AUTOBIOGRAPHY
2015   Arguments Yard (Cherry Red Books)
Plus many poems included in anthologies large and small

DISCOGRAPHY
All UK releases except where stated

SOLO
1981   Phasing Out Capitalism cassette (No Wonder)
1982   Rough, Raw and Ranting EP with Seething Wells (Radical Wallpaper)
1982   Cocktails EP (Cherry Red)
1983   Ranting at the Nation LP (Cherry Red)
1984   Sawdust and Empire LP (Anagram)
1984   Radio Rap! EP (Cherry Red)
1984   Livingstone Rap! EP (Cherry Red Ken)
1987   Libyan Students from Hell! LP (Plastic Head)
1988   Scornflakes LP/cassette (Probe Plus)
1990   (Canada) Live at the Rivoli LP/cassette (Festival)
1991   Donkey's Years CD/LP/cassette (Musidisc)
1992   (Germany) This Is Free Europe CD/LP/single (Terz)
1993   (Australia) 668-Neighbour of the Beast CD/cassette (Larrikin)
1993   (Germany) Live auf St.Pauli CD (Terz)
1993   Attila the Stockbroker's Greatest Hits cassette (Roundhead)
1999   Poems Ancient & Modern CD (Roundhead/Mad Butcher)
1999   The Pen & The Sword CD (Roundhead/Mad Butcher)

2003   Live in Belfast CD (Roundhead)
2007   (Norway) Spirit of Revolution vinyl EP with Patrik Fitzgerald (Crispin Glover)
2007   (Norway) Live In Norway CD (Crispin Glover)
2008   Spirit of the Age compilation CD (Roundhead)
2010   (Germany) Disestablished 1980 song compilation CD (Mad Butcher)
2012   The Long Goodbye/Never Too Late EP (Roundhead)
2015   Live at the Greys (Roundhead)
2020   (Finland) Heart On My Sleeve LP (Hiljaiset Levyt)

2004   DVD – Live at the Heartland Café

With JOHN OTWAY
1991   Cheryl - a Rock Opera CD/cassette (Strikeback)

With BARNSTORMER
1995   Renaissancecore cassette (Roundhead)
1995   (Germany) Sarajevo EP (Mad Butcher)
1996   The Siege of Shoreham CD/cass (Roundhead)
1998   Live in Hamburg cassette (Roundhead)
1999   (Germany) The Siege of Shoreham CD (Puffotter Platten) and LP (East Side Records)
2000   Just One Life (Roundhead)
2000   (Germany) Just One Life LP (Teenage Rebel Records)
2004   Zero Tolerance (Roundhead)
2004   (Germany) Zero Tolerance LP (East Side Records)
2004   Baghdad Ska - split single with Bomb Factory (Repeat Records)
2012   Bankers & Looters CD (Mad Butcher)
2012   (Holland) Bankers & Looters LP (Hupseeln Records)
2018   Restoration Tragedy CD/double LP as Barnstormer 1649 (Roundhead)

With SEAGULLS SKA
2005   Tom Hark (We Want Falmer) EP - Reached number 17 in the UK Top 40 on January 9th 2005 (Skint Records)

With CONTINGENT (Belgium) as bass player
2010   Destinee Fragile

CONTENTS

To My Wife In Lockdown 4

Foreword 15
Take Courage. 16
Lost in the Supermarket. 17

EARLY MEMORIES AND FAMILY
Poppy's Poem 18
Never Too Late 19
My Brother, Uncle Don 22
Auntie Rose 23
My Ninth Birthday 25
The Days on Burrow Hill. 30
The Long Goodbye 32
It's Made of Wire 43
Bottom Feeders 46

RECENT REALITIES
Stay Alert! 50
Love Your Lungs 51
Too Much Pressure 52
In Training 53
Candid Camera 55

MY ENGLAND (AND SCOTLAND)
Southwick 56
Missionaries. 58
Shed Fire 62
Slough 63
To Slough & Sanity 65
Worthing 66
Dustbin Poem 67
New Brighton 68
Stornoway 69

Harrogate	70
Braintree	72
Foyer Bar	75
Sealand	76

LITTLE ENGLAND

Asylum-Seeking Daleks	78
Take Back Control	80
Opinion Farm	81
Rock 'n' Roll Brexit	83
Every Time I Eat Vegetables	85
UK Gin Dependence Party	86
Poison Pensioner	88
Use of English	90
An In-Out Referendum On Europe	91
There's A Man Down Our Road Who's A Nazi	93
Thoughts on the 'March for England'	94
Xenophobia	95
Language Barrier	96
Keeping Up Appearances	98

FURTHER AFIELD

Mountaineering in Belgium	99
Canada Surprise	100
Australian Decomposition	101
Punk Night at the Duck's Nuts	102
Newcastle – The Replay	105

THE EARLY YEARS – 1980-85

They Must Be Russians	110
Russians in the DHSS	111
Russians in McDonald's	112
Russians at the Henley Regatta	113
Russians on the Centre Court	114

Russians vs the Tetley Bittermen 116
A Bang and a Wimpy. 119
Contributory Negligence 120
Awayday. 122
Nigel wants to go to C&A's 124
Nigel wants to go & see Simple Minds. 125
I Don't Talk to Pop Stars 126
The Night I Slept with Seething Wells 128
The Perils of Stealing Half a Bottle of Wine. 129
Gentlemen of the Wrist 130
My Wardrobe. 133
Death in Bromley 135
Video Nazis 136
Andy is a Corporatist. 137
The Oracle 139
A Very Silly East European Propaganda Station. 140

THE STATE OF THINGS
Trot Zombie Takeover Apocalypse. 142
Repossessed by the Devil 144
April Fool in September. 145
Never Forget 148
Theresa the Appeaser 150
A Tale Of Three Bushes 150
A Man Of His Word 151
My Doctor Martens. 152
Supermodel 155
A Hellish Encounter. 157
Carriage H 160
Attila the Stockbroker Cleans Up the City. 162
A Diet of Mainstream Media. 164
At No Parliamentary Expense 164
Undaunted. 165

A LOAD OF BELLOC'S
A Cautionary Tale 170
The Maggot. 172
The British Bullfrog. 173
The Rat-tailed Maggot 176

How Are Your Bins Doing In This Hot Weather? 177
The Crayfish. 178
The Axolotl 178
The Lugworm 179
The Slug. 180
The Lemming 181
The Don't Care Bear 182
Written from Scratch 183
Victoria Road 185

'JOURNALISM'
The Bible According To Rupert Murdoch 188
A Sugared Dish 189

DOMESTICITY
Two Glastonbury Errors. 190
A Hole Series 191
On Being Defrosted 193
A Nasal Appraisal. 194

THE SEETHING WELLS MEMORIAL SOCIAL SURREALIST SECTION
Coronavirus vs the Tetley Bittermen 196
Frogspawn Man vs the Boy Racers. 197
Beer Gardening 200
Designated Areas 201
Spam 204
North Korea Mourns Comrade Mickey Finn of T.Rex 206
668: Neighbour of the Beast 208
The Sack. 209
Fugazi, Cliff Richard & Me 212
The Social Surrealist Weapons Inspector's Report 214
The Mandelson Violin Concerto 216
The Zen Stalinist Manifesto. 217

SHORT & SWEET
The Marxist Tomato Grower 221
This Means Waugh 221
Rogered!. 221
The Ultimate Festival Toilet. 221

SAYING GOODBYE
Veronica 222
Two Cans Of Zywiec 228
Bob Crow 229
Red Wedgewood 230
Little Man, Big Heart 231

M.C. ATTILA
Coro Nation 235
Forty Years in Rhyme 237
Substitute 239
Talkin' Bout My Generation 242
Crime Writer 244
The Iron Men Of Rap! 246
Boys In The Hood 248
Radio Rap! 250
New World Order Rap 252
Tell Sid He'd Better Buy His Mum A Jumper 255
Comic in a Basket 257
Spirit of the Age 261

JUST PLAIN REVOLTING
Joseph Porter's Sleeping Bag 263
The Final Ablution 264
The Nuptual Fireplace 265
The Return of Winter Vomiting Bug 266

FOOTBALL
Goldstone Ghosts 268
From Hereford To Here 270
And Smith Must Score 272
Archer's Shame 273
A Symptom of Modern Society 274
The Leppings Lane End 275
Terms & Conditions 276
For Roy 277
Another Football Obscenity 278
A Pride of Seagulls 279
N-n-n-n- Nine Nil 280

SELECTED SONG LYRICS

Fifth Column	282
Sawdust & Empire	284
The Ballad Of Airstrip One	286
Libyan Students from Hell!	287
Market Sektor One	289
Tyler Smiles	290
This Is Free Europe	292
Sarajevo	294
Mohammed the Kabul Red	296
The Blandford Forum	298
Scumball Pinochet	300
Bicycle Testicle	301
Just One Life	302
Death of a Salesman	303
Hey Celebrity	305
Comandante Joe	307
Guy Fawkes' Table	308
Baghdad Ska	310
Valentine's Day	312
Looters	313
Bye Bye Banker	315
Mission Creep	317
Only Football	319
Pride's Purge	321
Wellingborough & Wigan	322
Abiezer Coppe	323
The Fisherman's Tale	325
Harrison	327
The Man With the Beard	329
Prince Harry's Knob	330
My Poetic Licence	332

ATTILA THE STOCKBROKER

In memory of Steven 'Seething' Wells, 1960-2009.
We started together.
He finished too soon.

FOREWORD

Today, September 8th, 2020 is the 40th anniversary of my first gig as Attila the Stockbroker, so this year seemed the perfect time to publish an anthology of all my best work over the past forty years. Little did I know what was in store.

I had booked a celebratory tour of Britain and Europe and was in the middle of selecting and working out an order for the huge quantities of poems and song lyrics I was planning to include in this book when suddenly the world changed. A pandemic of a size and power unknown since the Spanish flu epidemic of 1918 swept across the planet, bringing our everyday activities to a grinding halt.

Live gigs stopped. Everything non-essential stopped. We were confined to our homes for weeks on end as a Tory government instituted a level of state support unprecedented in the political history of this country to stop our national infrastructure from falling apart. The outpourings of solidarity from ordinary people moved me beyond belief. The complacency and arrogance of a few (including many in government) angered me beyond belief as well. And Dominic Cummings made me vomit.

I started doing gigs from my office on Facebook Live, reaching thousands of people and reconnecting with some who had loved my stuff years ago. Most were fund raisers for the brilliant 'We Shall Overcome' homeless initiative, local food banks or the 'FieldMe' group helping fellow performers rendered penniless by the cancellation of all live work. And I carried on compiling this book, with the nagging thought in my mind that due to the lung condition I had acquired through inhaling other people's smoke at gigs for more than two decades before the smoking ban, I was very vulnerable to the disease…

As I write, the pandemic is still with us. I want to get this finished quickly. It contains my very best poems and songs from 40 years earning my living doing something I love doing today even more than I did when I began. Simple as that.

Please enjoy my life's work. (So far, I hope!)

And huge thanks to the three brilliant cartoonists who have turned my words into pictures over the years – the multi-talented Phill 'Porky the Poet' Jupitus in the early days, Womble (aka Dave Trent) in the middle years and latterly the late, great Dan Woods, also guitarist in my band Barnstormer. Thanks also to biologist Nick Staples for the beautiful rat-tailed maggot and lugworm.

Attila, 2020

TAKE COURAGE (March 2020)

Another day. Two puffs on my inhaler.
My breathing calm and steady as before
No sudden cough, no temperature, I'm ready
To write and think and help for one day more
My big strong arms seek solace in the garden
My cycling legs flex slowly with regret
No pleasure in those rides along the coast path
When every fellow human is a threat.

I'm fit for 62, no doubt about it
Except my lungs, and that's no fault of mine
They bellowed me through some two thousand concerts
When all those cigarettes were thought just fine
They still fuel me for miles when I'm out cycling -
There's millions of folk far worse off than me!
I didn't feel such fear when I had cancer:
That pink mass in my bladder I could see.

The fear we feel is normal. Let's not hide it.
But don't let it supplant the love of life.
Do all you can to help the folk around you -
I see that courage in my steadfast wife.
And if the battle comes, well, now I'm ready
To take the bastard on with all my might.
And if I lose: you'll face a brand new future.
Please use my poems and songs to spread some light.

LOST IN THE SUPERMARKET

I don't want cashback
I want The Clash back.

2010

EARLY MEMORIES & FAMILY

POPPY'S POEM
For my father, Bill Baine, 1899-1968
1/15th Battalion, London Regiment, #535068, WW1

'What passing-bells for those who die as cattle?
Only the monstrous anger of the guns.'
And so some lines to spike centenary prattle:
These words a sole survivor soldier's son's.

My father Bill, born in Victorian England:
The sixth of January, 1899.
His stock, loyal London. Proletarian doff-cap.
Aged just eighteen, he went to join the line.

Not in a war to end all wars forever
But in a ghastly slaughter at the Somme -
A pointless feud, a royal family squabble
Fought by their proxy poor with gun and bomb.

My father saved. Pyrexia, unknown origin.
Front line battalion: he lay sick in bed.
His comrades formed their line, then came the whistle
And then the news that every one was dead.

In later life a polished comic poet
No words to us expressed that awful fear
Although we knew such things were not forgotten.
He dreamed Sassoon: he wrote Belloc and Lear.

When I was ten he died, but I remember,
Although just once, he'd hinted at the truth.
He put down Henry King and Jabberwocky
And read me Owen's 'Anthem For Doomed Youth'.

'What passing-bells for those who die as cattle?
Only the monstrous anger of the guns.'
And so some lines to spike centenary prattle:
These words a sole survivor soldier's son's.

2014

NEVER TOO LATE
For my stepfather, John Stanford

My father died when I was ten
and when she'd dried her tears
Mum met you in the choir -
she'd known of you for years
I was so pleased when she told me
that she would be your wife
and I looked forward happily
to a new man in my life

But you were the classical singer
who thought rock'n'roll was junk
and I was the Bolan boogie boy
who soon became a punk
You were the civil servant
for whom everything had its place
and I was the left wing activist
out there and in your face

Yes, you were the 'head of the household'
and I was the stroppy kid
We wound each other up for sure
We flipped each other's lid
But later we both learned so much
and something new began
And here's a poem I wrote for you
You decent, gentle man

So I went off to my own life
Left you and Mum to yours
A few words about football
Then the sound of closing doors
But the passing of so many years
gave us both time to reflect
And slowly, oh, so slowly,
we forged a new respect.

When you were ill the first time
and found it hard to walk
I'd take you to the hospital
and we would sit and talk
It felt so right and normal
And it was such a shame
that it had taken all this time -
Both stubborn, both to blame.

'Cos you were the 'head of the household'
and I was the stroppy kid
We wound each other up for sure
We flipped each other's lid
But later we both learned so much
and something new began
And here's a poem I wrote for you
You decent, gentle man

When Mum came down with Alzheimer's
Five years you cooked and cared
And we were round there every day
so many thoughts were shared
Your simple, honest loyalty
The vows you made, you'd keep
No longer the big boss man
Me, no longer the black sheep

Then came that day in hospital
The end was near, we knew
You told me 'I do love you John'
I said 'I love you too'
You took my hand and squeezed it
Our eyes were filled with tears
The first time that we'd said that -
It took thirty-seven years.

Heart On My Sleeve

'Cos you were the 'head of the household'
and I was the stroppy kid
We wound each other up for sure
We flipped each other's lid
But later we both learned so much
and something new began
And here's a poem I wrote for you
You decent, gentle man

It's never too late
never too late
never too late to say you love someone

And if it wasn't too late for me and John
Then it's never too late for anyone

2009

MY BROTHER, UNCLE DON
Donald Baine, 1929-2020
Elder son of our dad, Bill Baine, 1899-1968

End of an era. Goodbye 'Uncle Don'.
I've known you all my life and now you're gone.
My parents said that's what I should call you
When I was three and you were thirty-two
But soon I said, 'Mum, 'Uncle''s just polite.
Don's not my uncle. He's my brother, right?'
Soon this precocious kid just called you 'Don' -
For over fifty years. And now you're gone.

Yes, you were born in 1929.
Your generation precedent to mine.
A copper in the old George Dixon style
Who saw the Met change for the worse after a while
And left. A decent, caring family bloke.
We'd share a fishing trip and share a joke.
You didn't really 'get' the life I found -
That didn't stop us treading common ground.

Last time we spoke we knew the end was near.
You talked of death quite calmly, without fear.
Had over sixty years with your dear wife
Your kids and grand and great grandkids your life.
A life lived to the full till ninety-one.
This brother young enough to be your son
Salutes you, and the memories of our dad
Whose path you followed, and whose voice you had.

2020

AUNTIE ROSE

Auntie Rose
lived next door to us
here in Southwick.
Twenties flapper hat
Twenties clothes
Twenties shoes
...it was 1964.
Faded, but still glamourous.
Retired buyer
for Debenhams of Brighton.
Never married.
Every Tuesday
after primary school
I'd go round for tea.
Tinned herring roes on toast
Cheese and onion crisps
a game of snap
then home to bed.
Every Tuesday
I'd marvel at her outside toilet
with the big spiders
her garden
with the stag beetles
her living room
with furniture from a bygone age
and a grandfather clock
from an even more bygone age
and her mantelpiece
crammed with stuff.
There were two pictures on it.
One of her as a little girl
standing with the Southwick football team
in the 1890s
and one of a man
standing in a field
leaning on a rifle.

Attila The Stockbroker

I'd always wondered
so one day, aged about eight,
I asked the question.
'Auntie Rose,
Why did you never get married?'

She smiled
and pointed to the photo.

'The man in the photo
is the man I was going to marry.
He was killed in the First World War.
I never loved anyone else
So I never got married, John.
That's why'.

I looked at her.
'That's really sad, Auntie!'
She smiled bravely.
We had another game of snap.

2012

MY NINTH BIRTHDAY
For the people of Aberfan, 50 years on. One of my most powerful early memories and a day I shall never forget.

I'm sure it won't surprise you to learn
I was a proper little show-off.
'Too clever by half'
said my Victorian grandmother
who lived in the flat downstairs.
'You spoil him, Muriel.
Children should be seen
and not heard.
Be quiet, John!
When you begin to PAY a little
Then you can begin to SAY a little.'
There were plenty more such epithets.
If I asked what was for tea
on the days she was in charge of me
she'd always say
'Air pie and a walk round'
or 'Bread and pullet'
and when she read about the latest exploits
of the royal family
or anyone else remotely wealthy or privileged
in the pages of her beloved Daily Express
she'd often exclaim with heartfelt approval
'It's not for the likes of us!'
(When, years later, I read
'The Ragged Trousered Philanthropists'
by Robert Tressell
and heard that particular servile catchphrase again
I felt retrospectively vindicated
in my instinctive determination back then
to do the exact opposite
of nearly everything she told me.)

Despite my grandmother's best efforts
I was seen, heard
and then some -

in school and out.
Self-assured and confident.
Playing the violin and recorder.
Writing little poems and songs
and about to begin a massive project
about the American Civil War
based on the battle stories printed on the back
of the unbelievably gory bubblegum picture cards
we boys bought on our way to school.
Cards with titles like 'Crushed By The Wheels'
'Wall of Corpses'
and 'Messenger of Death.'
(If you're male and over 50, you'll probably remember)
My form teacher liked me
and let me help other kids in class.
I had lots of friends
and if wannabe bullies hit me
I hit them back.

Like I say, a proper little show-off.

It was my ninth birthday.
At Manor Hall Junior School
when it was your birthday
you couldn't wait till lunchtime -
but you had to.
Then you stood in front of everyone else
in the canteen
a big, colourful plastic cake was brought out
with proper candles on it
you blew out the candles
everyone sang 'Happy Birthday'
(even the kids who thought you were a show-off wanker:
the teachers made sure of that)
and you got the chance to grab a handful of sweets
from a big jar.
As far as I can remember
I was the only one
with a birthday that day

so I had everyone's undivided attention.
I was really looking forward to it.
But I never got to show off
and I didn't want to show off.
My ninth birthday was different.
It was October 21st, 1966.

Before we went to the canteen for lunch
and my little birthday cameo
we were told there was going to be a special assembly
in the school hall.
Everyone wondered what had happened:
even I realised they wouldn't have one
just because it was my birthday.
The headmaster, Mr. Young,
came in looking very sad
and told us that earlier that day
a huge mountain of coal waste
had engulfed a junior school like ours
in a Welsh mining village called Aberfan
and many children the same age as us
had lost their lives.
He asked us to pray for them.
We all did.
Some of us cried.
They still sang 'Happy Birthday'
in the canteen
a few minutes later
but it wasn't a happy birthday at all.
I kept thinking about those children.
After I'd got home
and talked to my parents
and had my birthday tea with my friends
I tried to write a poem for Aberfan -
but I couldn't.
The poem I wanted to write
was far too big for a nine year old.
We did a collection at school
the money was sent to the disaster fund

and then
as happens when you're a child
with loving parents
at a supportive school
other things quickly came along
to take the sadness away.
But on my birthday
for the next few years
I always thought
about the children of Aberfan.

Years later, I learned
about the underground springs
below Colliery Waste Tip No 7
on the hill above the village
which caused the coal waste to turn to slurry
and crash down on the school -
springs easily spotted on maps
which were never even consulted.
I learned about the negligence
of the authorities
and the insensitivity of the press.
Some things never change.
I learned about the father who -
as the inquest into his child's death
declared the cause to be 'asphyxia and multiple injuries' -
shouted out
'No, sir. Buried alive by the National Coal Board.'
I learned how a ruling was made
that parents had somehow to prove
their childrens' deaths had caused them anguish
before they could benefit
from the disaster fund -
and that some of the money
from that fund
was used to clear the other waste tips
above Aberfan
because the Coal Board
refused to pay for it to be done.

I learned about the long-term psychological effects
of the disaster
on the whole village.
In short
I learned how the lives
of working class people
– of working class children –
were held cheap...
So cheap.

But that was much later.
Back then
I was a child.
A proper little show-off
who didn't want to show off
on his ninth birthday
trying to write a poem
for children like him –
for the children
of Aberfan.

2016

THE DAYS ON BURROW HILL

For my late niece Sally. Written, with much love, Xmas 2013.
Dedicated to her sons Ben and Jamie, both fellow musicians.

Now it's two days before Christmas
Winter wind roars wild and cold
And I'm thinking of you, Sally,
And those memories of old
Fifty years have been and gone now
But my mind it lingers still
On those happy times in Plymstock -
Summer days on Burrow Hill.

I would always so look forward
To those yearly trips down West
Mum and Poppy off together
For a short, much-needed rest
While their stroppy little offspring
With a voice both loud and shrill
Went to stay with 'Auntie' Audrey -
Right next door to Burrow Hill.

Sue and Dave were eight or nine then
You and I were six or seven
When we first slipped out the back door
And ran off to slow worm heaven...
Lifting stones and bits of metal
Catching lizards with great skill
Cabbage whites were ten a penny
In those days on Burrow Hill.

Heart On My Sleeve

Then the older ones stopped coming
And it was just you and me
With our box of scaly trophies
Running back home for our tea
Summer melted into summer -
Each year we went back, until
Puberty and land developers
Saw the end of Burrow Hill.

But I still have three pet corn snakes
Staring at me beady-eyed
And I still lift up old tree trunks
Wife Robina by my side
And two newts, bought from your pet shop,
On my desk, remind me still
Of those happy days of childhood -
Summer days on Burrow Hill.

2013

THE LONG GOODBYE

I wrote this poem during the last stages of my mother Muriel's six year battle with Alzheimer's to help her remember who she was. It was inspired by her many insightful comments on how it felt to be in the grip of that awful disease, and it is dedicated to all those whose lives have also been touched by it.

This is a poem for you, Mum.
It's about your long, eventful life,
the you that you were
and the you that you are now,
the different you,
the you with Alzheimer's.
It's to help you remember.
And, yes, I knew when I was writing this
that it was to help me, too.
So this is a poem for us, Mum.

You say
'It's like wading through treacle
and when I get through the treacle
there's a mist
which makes me wonder
why I bothered with the treacle.'

But there are places we can go
in the hours we spend together
where there is no treacle
no mist -
where everything is clear.

Back to Gravesend
to the council house
to the stern, Victorian printer father
and the spirited, intelligent little girl
who went to Reading for the holidays
to stay with your 'maiden aunt', a teacher
and discovered a new, magical world -
the piano.
Auntie Evelyn paid for your lessons

and your talent blossomed.
Church organist at 16.
And not just in music:
A scholarship to the county grammar school
Matriculation...
and then came the war.

You say
'It's as though bits of my mind are still awake,
and bits have gone to sleep
or start imagining things'.

You were sent to Bletchley Park.
You mostly can't remember what happened yesterday
but you can still describe every corridor at Bletchley,
the walks through the town
and, of course, the hours at the piano
in the music room.
Typing through the night
on one of the Enigma decoding machines
Smoking to stay awake –
you've always hated smoking –
and the bustle and uproar
when the nonsense you were typing
suddenly turned to German
and the 'boffins' gathered round you, urging you on.
'Faster! Faster!'
Your three friends:
Jean, Margaret, Win.
Still friends, nearly seventy years later.
When the mist is all around
I say 'Tell me about Bletchley Park'.
In an instant, I have my Mum back.

You say
'I am learning the difference
between understanding and memory.
I can still speak, still form sentences,
talk to people,

read the Guardian and enjoy it.
Though I don't remember what I have read
or what I have said.
In one ear, out the other!
But if my memory is gone, how is it that
I remember
how to understand?'

After Bletchley: London.
Notting Hill.
Working at Bateman's Opticians
in Kensington High Street.
Singing with the Royal Choral Society
under Malcolm Sergeant
premiering the works of Elgar.
The music appreciation class
where you met my father
Twenty five years your senior
living in a hostel
on the run from a brutal marriage.
You brought the sunshine back into his life
And when the divorce made the national press
as a legal precedent
you didn't care:
you were one.
Visiting the Isle of Harris
Honeymoon in Switzerland
My father's love poems to you.
Yes, that's where I got this from.
You tell me over and over again...
The words from him;
the music from you.
Ok, not exactly in the way you'd have expected -
Rude words!
Loud music!
But you're used to that now.
(You've had more than thirty years of it,
after all!)

Heart On My Sleeve

You say
'I know the meaning of the phrase
'a fate worse than death'.'

Come on, Mum.
You're at home, in your warm, comfortable house in Southwick
We live just round the corner
I'm here, my wife Robina's here, family and friends are here...
You could be in Baghdad or Kabul
Family killed, cowering in a ruined cellar
Not knowing who or where you were...
It's not that bad!

You say
'You're right, John. I mustn't be so silly'.
Together we smile and sing
'Always look on the bright side of life!'
I go and make you a cup of tea.
I bring it to you.

You say
'I know the meaning of the phrase
'a fate worse than death'.'

Of course, I'm used to the repetition.
But I'll never get used to that one.

Now we're moving into the fifties
and here's the treacle.
You can't remember
the year I was born.
'How can I forget that?'
Then with great authority:
'NINETEEN FORTY-SEVEN!'

Hang on, Mum...
You weren't married till fifty–three
And though I am a bit of an old git

I'm not THAT much of an old git.
It was FIFTY-seven.

Tears fill your eyes.
'How can I forget that?
I remember you as a little boy.
Always questioning. Always loud.
'No, Mummy!!'
'Why, Mummy??"

Too right!

You say
'I have spent my life doing.
But now I'm just... being.'

The move to Southwick when I was three.
The worms, then the fish, lizards, slow worms,
newts, terrapins, snakes.
Going to football every week with my father
And the one time I heard you argue.
Do you remember why it was?
That's right.
He'd left his Brighton season ticket
in his trouser pocket.
You put the trousers in the washing machine...
We both laugh.

You say
'Memory is such a wonderful thing.
But you don't appreciate that
until it's disappearing.
My brain feels like a sponge
with great big holes in it.'

I tell you how clever you are
to use that analogy
because if you look at a photograph
of the brain of a person with Alzheimer's

that's exactly what it looks like –
a sponge
with great big holes in it.
Sometimes you say your brain feels like soup,
or suet pudding, or sausages,
But mostly it's a sponge.
A thirsty sponge, full of life
which soaked up everything it possibly could
for more than eighty years
and is now, gently, leaking it away.

You say:
'I love you, my son.
You are my rock!'
I say
I love you too, Mum.
I'm your punk rock.

Then the difficult years:
My father's death when I was ten
(yes, it was 1968, Mum...
I know it feels like a lifetime
- it's half of one)
My battles with school
and a new stepfather
and so away, to university,
to the world of punk rock,
to a band and a squat in Brussels,
a flat in Harlow Town
with my friend Steve
and, in 1980,
to a life as Attila the Stockbroker...
a life you tried hard to understand
and discussed with me late into the night
on my visits home.
A life you always encouraged
and were proud of
and, on a few memorable occasions,
came to share.

As we will see.

Of course, you had your own life.
Very different from mine!
Organist at three churches
Teaching the piano
Singing with the Brighton Festival Chorus
Playing with Southwick Operatic Society
President of Southwick W.I.
(Remember the gig I did for your W.I?
'You must ask your son to come and read for us, Muriel...'
You were very worried.
I'm not surprised!
I chose my material, erm, carefully.
I got an encore.)

And, in 1981,
you'd won your first big battle:
Breast cancer.

You say
'Alzheimer's is such a cruel disease.
You can have your breast removed –
But not your head.
That's a shame!'

The surgeon prodded your breast, and said
'That'll have to come off.'
His exact words.
So angered and devastated were you
by his unbelievable insensitivity
that, after your mastectomy
and your recovery
(via New Zealand, where you went to see your brother –
'If this is going to kill me
I'm going to see Mick in New Zealand first')
you started a local counselling service
for people with cancer.
Especially women with breast cancer.

Especially women with breast cancer
dealing with insensitive male bastards.
You knew.
You helped so many people.
And I was so proud of you.

You say 'Time is all out of joint.
Things that happened yesterday
seem a long time ago
and things that happened a long time ago
seem like yesterday.
That is frightening'.

Now we're nearing the 90s
and we're knee deep in treacle.
Remember Canada, Mum?
Not really? I'll remind you.
1989.
You said 'I'll come with you!
My old Bletchley friend Win
lives in Toronto...'
And you did.
I was touring, 11 cities,
east to west.
You stayed with Win in Toronto
then joined me on tour
all the way to Vancouver.
'Hey, Attila's brought his mom with him!'
You played piano for me
on my song 'Tyler Smiles'
at the Vancouver Folk Festival
to a standing ovation
and enjoyed it so much
that two years later
you toured New Zealand with me
saw your brother Mick again -
and then to Australia.
'Strewth, Attila's brought his mum with him!'
They thought it'd be fun

for you to interview me
on national TV
on the beach
next to a sewage outfall.
You were brilliant.

You say
'I feel as though I am moving slowly
down a road
which is gently subsiding'.

Your swan song
with the Brighton Festival Chorus.
Elgar's 'Dream of Gerontius'
at the Royal Festival Hall.
Mum's last gig.
Your favourite piece of music, ever.
I was there.

Then, in 1998,
your final tour with me,
my favourite memory of all:
Germany.
'I've never been to Germany, John.
I want to go there before I die.
I want to talk to the people there.
All this prejudice in my generation
is just silly'.
But Mum, I said.
It won't be like those other tours.
I've told you about Germany.
I play in anti-fascist squats and autonomous centres.
We sleep on the floor half the time.
Sometimes it's really cold and very smoky
there is loads of very loud punk rock
and everyone drinks the most INCREDIBLE amount of beer.
Including me -
ESPECIALLY me!
I'm not sure it's the right tour
For a lady of seventy-five…

Heart On My Sleeve

But you were having none of it.
So off we went.
You, me, Adverts punk legend TV Smith
and Danny the driver
in my old Citroen
charging up and down the motorway.
I'd told the organisers –
and they were brilliant.
They made such a fuss of you.
Clean, comfortable and warm everywhere
no smoke
and punk rock turned down where necessary.
Most solicitous of all
my old mate
Mad Butcher Mike –
a big, hard, red skinhead,
founder of a legendary hardcore anti-fascist record label,
loathed by every right wing scumbag in Germany.
You took a real shine to him.
And he to you.
'He's not a Mad Butcher at all, John –
He's a very nice chap!'

Germany was your last foray.
You sailed into your eighties,
happy in Southwick.
I'd moved nearby years before
Then married Robina.
She spotted the signs before I did -
I guess I simply couldn't believe
it would happen to you.
And then came that fateful day
in May 2004
when you set out in the car
to visit Daphne, your sister in law
and forgot where you were going
or why you were going there.

It's been more than five years now:
and here we are.
The psychiatrist says you're doing very well
That the tablets are working
That we're doing all the right things
That the hours we spend are precious hours...
We know that.
I know that.
I see it in your face, every time I enter the room.
Your indomitable spirit,
your need for human warmth,
for company, for stimulation
for mental challenge
is as strong as ever.
Anyway, for me, no contest.
You made me. You need me. I'll be there. That's it.
But it's hard, Mum.
For us, and, above all, for you.
Which is why I wrote this poem.
To help you remember.
The poem of your life –
The poem of our life.

Mum died on June 9th, 2010, the day before her 87th birthday.
Her last words to me were 'Have a good gig'.
Thanks, Mum.
I am.

2009

IT'S MADE OF WIRE

It's made of wire.
No, let's be more specific.
It's a piece of wire.
A piece of wire twisted round itself
with a loop at the far end.
It looks like a stiff metal lasso.
There's an egg slicer too,
some plastic moulds
to make pastry shapes
and a brush thing:
it's not a brush,
it's a thing that looks like a brush,
but you couldn't possibly use it as a brush
because it's two inches across
and the bristles are two inches long
and a quarter of an inch wide.
(I suppose you could use it to brush spilt salt
into a neat pile
or, if you were a masochist,
to dust a room, very, very slowly:
but that would be just silly.)

They are in a forgotten drawer
in my late mother's kitchen.
We are clearing the house.

Suddenly I am seven years old again.
Lassoing a boiled egg with the wire noose
and burning my fingers
as I try to manoeuvre it into the egg cup
- I was as cack-handed then
as I am now -
or burning them even more
when I peel the egg while it is too hot,
so I can experience the wild, destructive delight
of forcing it through the ridiculously inefficient egg slicer
and watching the bits go everywhere.

Stabbing the pastry with the mould
Grabbing the shape
Sprinkling some sugar on it
and running into my bedroom to eat it raw.
Raw pastry with sugar sprinkled on it: 1
Jamie Oliver: 0.
No contest.

And the brush?
Mum painted the pastry with it.
I thought it was odd
to paint food with a brush
but it always tasted good
so I didn't care.

The wire lasso
and the plastic shapes
and the egg slicer
go into a carrier bag.
One of many carrier bags
which go into black sacks
which go into the back of my car
which goes to the tip.
At the tip
I empty the other bags first:
Dusty flower arranging stuff
Faded dressmaking patterns
Old W.I magazines
Rotas for Mum's cancer counselling group
that stopped years ago:
all the residue of a long life
we can't possibly find homes for
and, given the mementoes I have already selected,
it would be pointless to keep.
As the last bag
with the kitchen stuff in it
hits the floor of the skip
it carries a little bit of me with it
and the next morning

Heart On My Sleeve

I wish I had saved the wire lasso
and the egg slicer
and the funny brush thing
- and that is ridiculous.

It is ridiculous, isn't it.
Isn't it?

Anyway, I wrote this poem instead.
I've saved them here.
I feel better now.

2010

BOTTOM FEEDERS

From the moment I could walk, I have always been fascinated by what many people rather dismissively call 'creepy crawlies' – reptiles, amphibians and insects. On my desk, as I write this, four fire-bellied toads are croaking at each other in one tank while two paddle-tailed newts lurk like prehistoric relics in the other. To my right my three pet corn snakes, Napoleon, Josephine and Emma, are dozing in their vivarium. If I see a piece of corrugated iron or something similar lying long forgotten on some old bit of waste ground I will always lift it up in the hope that a scaly or amphibian treasure is lurking beneath – and, happily, my wife Robina grew up doing exactly the same thing, so if you are out for a stroll and you see a middle-aged couple acting strangely on a bit of crappy, deserted scrubland lifting up lumps of old metal or pieces of rotten tree, it's probably us.

From my first glimpse of one while playing there as a small child, the steps and the grassy area by the houseboats on Shoreham beach were always known to me as 'the lizard place' and in the summer I would pester my parents to take me there as often as I could so I could catch some unsuspecting specimens, bring them home in a Tupperware box, stick them in my tank and feed them worms. There are loads of lizards by the houseboats today, so I obviously didn't cause any long term damage to the population. And in any case, when I was little I had such awful hay fever that my parents tried to keep me away from the long grass by the houseboats and preferred to let me do my investigating on Kingston beach, a couple of hundred yards from our Southwick home.

And thus, by the age of about four, I was also seriously into rock pools, crustaceans and fish. My long-suffering dad would hold my reins and clamber with me onto the 'threepenny bit' – the platform at the end of Shoreham harbour's middle pier at Kingston beach – so I could watch the anglers. I caught blennies in the rock pools. Then I got my first fishing rod for my birthday, and was (occasionally quite literally) hooked.

Neither of my parents shared my fascination, so by the age of about ten I was let loose on my own, with carefully prescribed limits.

'Don't mess around on the harbour arm, and don't let the big boys give you any of their cider. Don't fish on the hot water pipe behind the power station. It's dangerous.

Don't fish on the sewage outfall. It's dangerous AND disgusting. Yes, I know the other boys do, but that doesn't mean you can. It's revolting.'

'But Mum, that's where I caught all those big flounders we had for dinner the other day...'

It's not for nothing that flatfish are known as 'bottom feeders'.

In those days the harbour wasn't the corporate, fenced in, health and safety obsessed Fort Knox it is today, and you could wander in and out of anywhere and plead ignorance if someone shouted at you. So by my early teens I was trying out different fishing spots on both sides of the lock gates, from Aldrington Basin in the canal all the way to the end of the East Arm breakwater at the tip of the harbour. If I found a good spot, I'd leave a marker there so I knew where to come back to. And one school holiday when I was fifteen I found a really good spot in the canal. Big tasty flounders, eels, and loads of those unwanted scavengers, the sea angler's curse, the shore crab. 'I wonder what's down there?' I thought.

Soon I got my answer. It was a bike gang member called Clive. He'd been in some kind of feud, and a rival gang had given him some concrete socks and thrown him in. A big ship came through, and the propeller wash brought him to the surface. Recycled protein, of course, but I didn't tell my mum where those fish had come from...

Then, in 1974, our little bit of Sussex coast made headline news when Tory Prime Minister Edward Heath's yacht Morning Cloud sank off Shoreham with the loss of two crew members. I was fishing off the harbour arm and hooked something huge and more or less immobile – but not quite. Eventually it came free. On my hook was a mess of something which looked horribly like human hair. I have to say that that did really spook me - but it didn't stop me fishing. And up until the mid Eighties the fishing round here was really good – not just my favourites, the flatfish, but bass, mullet, black bream and the ubiquitous mackerel.

Strange but true: catching mackerel got me horribly pissed a couple of times. In the cold war seventies, Soviet ships came into port bringing softwoods from Archangel in the Baltic. Politics meant that the sailors weren't allowed to go into Southwick to the pubs – all they could do was walk along the harbour arm, chaperoned by their commissar. Despite months at sea they had no fresh fish on board, and they'd swap vodka for mackerel: absolutely disgusting and ludicrously strong vodka totally unlike anything a teenager (who up until that point had gleefully downed anything alcoholic he could get his hands on) had ever tasted before. A couple of sessions of extended regurgitation on the harbour arm sowed the seeds of a lifelong loathing of spirits and a devotion to the glories of beer. Thanks, comrades!

The mackerel are still here, but gill netters and factory fishing have decimated everything else, and these days I go more to celebrate my lifelong love of the sea than in any great expectation of a huge haul. But there are always surprises in store. Once I hooked something I assumed from its weight and behaviour pattern to be a huge lump of weed. As it reached the side of the harbour arm I saw it was some kind of green cloth. When I finally managed to hoist it up, I realized it was a Subbuteo pitch. Not wanting to upset the local piscine table football league, I threw it back.

And it was while fishing on the East Arm of Shoreham Harbour that I had one of the happiest moments of my life.

I've always combined fishing and music, occasionally to the irritation of my fellow anglers. Most species of fish feed best at night, and therefore one of my constant companions through the Seventies and Eighties was the John Peel Show on Radio One. Standing there, gazing across the sea at the lights of Brighton in the distance, thinking my own thoughts and taking in whatever eclectic mixture the great man decided to feed through my tinny little transistor.

So it was that night in March 1982. My first EP, 'Rough Raw & Ranting', a double A side with my comrade in ranting verse Seething Wells, had just been released. I was fishing and listening to Peelie. A record came to an end. I was engrossed in my own thoughts, but I heard him talking. Then he quite clearly said: 'Here's Attila the Stockbroker'.

I nearly dropped my rod in the sea.

I stood on the harbour arm, transfixed, trembling in disbelief, while John Peel played 'Russians in the DHSS' from our EP. I felt like I'd just scored the winning goal for Brighton in the Cup Final. A few minutes later, before I'd really taken it in, he played 'A Bang & A Wimpy.' I felt like I'd just scored the winning goal for us in the European Cup Final. Sitting here, writing this, that feeling has come back. It's a feeling I can't describe. A feeling that, literally, thousands of musicians and writers have had over the years.

That first play on the John Peel Show. The stuff of dreams!

Nobody, anywhere in the history of UK popular culture, has done so much for people trying to realise their ambitions and get their words and music across to the world. He did it for me: 2 sessions, loads of plays. Thanks to him I got the start which has enabled me to earn my living for 40 years doing what I love. He died, so tragically, at the height of his powers.

I'll never forget that night on the Southwick arm.
Thanks, Peelie.

2013, updated slightly

RECENT REALITIES

STAY ALERT!

Firstly, two written during the coronavirus pandemic.
A response to Johnson's ridiculous slogan to deal with the threat from a microscopic virus..

Stay alert!
It's huge and fat!
It's got a flicknife
And baseball bat!
Stay alert!
Like a pink thistle!
An album cover
By Throbbing Gristle!
Stay alert!
It's got a willy!
Waves it around!
Looks rather silly!
But don't be fooled –
Those pink spikes hurt!
So keep your eyes peeled.
Stay alert!

2020

LOVE YOUR LUNGS

And as coronavirus raged, and human lungs were in peril, the planet must have breathed a sigh of relief.

My little lungs are rather damaged
The planet's big lungs are the same
We both are in need of assistance:
In both cases, our species to blame.
I hope my lungs get through this crisis
But this really is not about me
It's the planet's great big lungs which matter
Because its lungs are our lungs, you see.
At the moment, the planet's inhaling
As its sore lungs fill up with clean air
If we learn what we must from this crisis
It won't matter if my lungs aren't there.

2020

TOO MUCH PRESSURE
(written just before my 50th birthday)

This angry young man is still angry, but older -
And now Father Time has just pissed on my shoulder.
'You've got to grow up, John - you're way past that stage!
You've reached the condition they call 'middle age'.
It's time to be quiet, say 'yes', watch TV -
High spot of the week, a nice dinner party
Polite conversation until you doze off
The topics: house prices, taxation and goff.
(That's golf, by the way, in case you're unsure -
Not pale folk in graveyards obsessed by The Cure)
Now just look at you in your Seventies gear
With your punk rock and football and microbrew beer
Political poems and loud, angry songs
You still want to change things and right the world's wrongs?
You stand up and shout and you get in a rage:
It's really not right in a man of your age.
On top of all that, and I don't mean to frighten -
Worst of all for your blood pressure: you support Brighton!
They're not very good and you don't want to die
So sit on the couch and watch Chelsea on Sky...'

NO!!!!!!!!!!!!!!!

Sure, I'll take the tablets, and drink a bit less.
If you fancy a game, I might play you at chess.
I hope that I'll make it till I'm ninety-five.
But one thing's for sure, Death - you'll take me alive!

2007

IN TRAINING
Dedicated to my wife Robina and to the NHS

I've always loved cycling -
but never as much as today.
Forty miles through the Sussex countryside
on a beautiful Spring afternoon.
In training.
Testing myself
like a boxer preparing his body for the fight.
Fitness helps post-surgical healing, they told me
and alcohol hinders it
so I've given up beer until after the operation.
In our criminally overstretched and underfunded NHS
with so many people in need
this red rocker
doesn't want to be a bed blocker
even for one day.
They'll know after the biopsy:
It's the wait, the not knowing, that's the worst.
Like back in the old days of the 80s
when we knew the fascists were going to attack the gig
but we didn't know whether there would be
a pathetic gaggle of scrawny 18 year olds
high on glue
one with 'Oi' tattooed on his forehead the wrong way round
'cos he'd done a DIY job in the mirror
or a big gang of the really hard bastards
all DMs, tattoos and nazi salutes.
During the day
it's OK, more or less:
I have a full life
and can mostly put things to the back of my mind
but at night
I wake to that same, recurring dark thought
and sheer human fear takes hold.
Then your warm arms embrace me
your soft breasts enclose me
your lips meet mine
we hold each other tight
your bush against my leg

and I am whole again.
It is a wonder and an honour to be this loved
especially given my regular deficiencies
in matters of etiquette, self-effacement, you name it -
and I return it
with all the force of my being.
I love you so much.
I know how hard it is for you too.
Thank you for being there.
My heart goes out to those
who have to face such things on their own
and my deepest respect
to the people whose profession
is to help them to do so.
Like all those at the core
of our wonderful NHS
they are the ones to be celebrated
- the real 'celebrities' -
not some vapid dork off a game show.
They need your vote
and your campaigning.
Victory to the junior doctors.
Long live the NHS!

I've always loved cycling –
but never as much as today.
Forty miles through the Sussex countryside
on a beautiful Spring afternoon.
In training.
Testing myself
like a boxer preparing his body for the fight.
Blood coursing,
Legs pumping,
Muscles flexing,
Thoughts racing.
Bursting with Life.

2015

CANDID CAMERA
An Ode to Flexible Cystoscopy

I know I sometimes can be
A loud-mouthed, stroppy prat
I know I'm a control freak
(And a bossy one at that)
My wife says when I'm eating
I am a total slob -
I'm still not sure that I deserved
A camera up my knob.

The poor thing shrivelled up in fear
Till it was hardly there
A tiny little pimple
In a nest of pubic hair
The camera made its entrance
The pain cut like a knife
And then I saw my bladder
For the first time in my life.

I'm glad that it went up there
Though sad at what it found
And it can come back anytime
To help me stay around
So three cheers for the NHS
And to that camera crew -
And if you're feeling odd 'down there'
You get it checked out too.

2015

MY ENGLAND
(and Scotland)

SOUTHWICK

Southwick is like Amsterdam
only smaller and quieter
there aren't any prostitutes or sex shops
New Model Army have never played here
very few people use illicit substances
and no one commits adultery.
Southwick is like Amsterdam
except that when you walk through the Square
the people who ask you for money
have perms instead of dreadlocks
'crack' is something found in the pavements
that the nice Adur Council workmen missed
'heroine' is strictly an amateur dramatic role
and 'pavement' is a pavement,
not a cultishly successful
American grunge band.
'Score' is something Southwick Football Club used to do
and hopefully will soon do again
'gay' means 'light-hearted or merry'
and 'dope' is someone
who has left their bus pass at home.
Terry and June have always lived in Southwick
Richard Briers thinks it's very nice
Monty Python visit occasionally
The Levellers' latest CD was spotted on sale in Woolworths once
and all the poets and socialists were turned back at Hove.
Except us.
I guessed we slipped through the net.
Southwick is like Amsterdam
except the power station only has one chimney
the second amputated, along with its body
in a very radical architectural mastectomy
and there's only one canal

but it does have rats though -
you can see them scurrying
around the jetties at dusk
which is lovely
and it's full of mullet in the summer
and quite a lot of flatfish too
which for a lover of flatfish like myself
if you mullet over
constitutes a ray of hope
since it's actually rather a brill and soleful
plaice
to write poetry
and there's a towpath
where you can skate too
if you're a dab hand at it
but be careful not to flounder over the edge
because the water is rather foul
and in September
there's often nearly as much scum on its surface
as there is at the Brighton Centre
just along the road
attending the Conservative Party Conference.
Southwick is like Amsterdam.
OK, Anne Frank didn't live here
and there aren't as many bicycles
and the Heineken's a lot weaker
and Ajax would be a little out of place in the Sussex County League
but we've got a lot more flatfish.
And where there are flatfish
there's poetry.

1996

(This was written 24 years ago. Southwick is very different now. There are loads of socialists – we're not far off taking control of the local council for literally the first time in history. I suspect one or two people may have been a bit extramarital, 'dope' definitely means 'skunk', and Woolworths is a wonderful Chinese supermarket.)

MISSIONARIES

Even when I was a kid
it always seemed a bit of a rough pub.
Red brick, foursquare, slightly shabby
On the seafront
just down from Southwick station
surrounded by the flats which had been built
on the land cleared
when most of the Victorian seafront community
where my grandad was born
was demolished in the Sixties.
Next to the Old Town Hall
Near the entrance to Shoreham Port
and the customs building.
The Pilot.
As far as I can remember
I'd only been in there once.
They say first impressions are lasting ones
and my first impression was
that if you wanted a pint of something
that definitely wasn't real ale
or a fight
or some of the stuff Lance Armstrong liked
or you wanted to get served
despite barely having pubic hair
or you'd been thrown out of all the other pubs in Southwick
or you were a lost sailor
just arrived in port
and desperate to get pissed
it was the place to be.

Anyway, as times grew harder
it gradually got more and more dilapidated
till it looked positively desolate –
Southwick's own Heartbreak Hotel -
and then, finally,
like so many of its fellows
in this land blighted by totally avoidable poverty
it closed.

Heart On My Sleeve

It had never meant anything to me
but I was still sad to see a pub close
in my local community
and so I was pleased
when, walking the dog
one day not long afterwards,
I spotted a new, bright blue sign on the front.
On it was a symbol
which looked like a fat blue seagull
plummeting to earth.
Brilliant, I thought.
Some Albion beer monster fans
are opening a new brewpub in Southwick!
The Fat Blue Seagull Brewery, maybe?
But when I got nearer I saw
that round the fat blue seagull
were the words
'Redeemed Christian Church of God
Kingdom Life Assembly
Achievers' Centre.'
Bloody hell, I said to myself:
The Pilot wasn't much of a pub –
but even it
didn't deserve that.
Taken over by a religious sect.
A pretty hardcore one too.
Among the list of activities on the board:
'4 hour night vigil
10pm-2am
every second Friday of the month'.
Now THERE's a way to show the locals a good time
on a Friday night...
Although on reflection
I did think that
four hours spent at the Pilot
even under this new management
would actually be preferable to a similar amount of time
spent there in the old days.

It'll last five minutes,
I thought
as I wandered past.
Congregation of zero.
It's true that Southwick
has a long established ecumenical scene
(my wife and mother both big players back in the day)
but I doubt that they'll have much to do
with a weird sect
based in a dodgy pub
on what is for many of them quite literally
the other side of the tracks.
If it's lucky
The Redeemed Christian Church of God
will be noticed sufficiently
for a few local kids
to spray some inaccurately drawn male genitalia
on its front door.

But then the place opened
and one Sunday, walking the dog,
I met them –
definitely making an impact
in our still more or less monocultural coastal village.
Loads of young black men and women
immaculately dressed in Sunday best
walking confidently down Southwick Street
wandering round Southwick shopping centre
smiling broadly
handing out leaflets.
The congregation
of a church founded in Nigeria
with branches all over England
and now, one in Southwick.
I took a leaflet.
'Welcome to Southwick' I said.
'Though don't try converting me
cos I'm a Marxist-Leninist.'

I thought of the irony.
Hey, Dr Livingstone,
what goes around comes around!
'How are you getting on?' I asked.
'Natives friendly?'
'Ok' they said.
But a few weeks later
they'd gone.
Moved to an estate in Fishersgate
a mile away.
Maybe it was me.
'Southwick? No chance.
Hotbed of Marxism-Leninism.'

Anyway, there are missionaries
in Fishersgate now.
It's one of the most deprived areas in the country.
It needs help.
Personally, I don't think it needs
The Redeemed Christian Church of God
any more than Africa
needed Dr. Livingstone
but maybe they'll do some good.
And at the very least
they should find it a bit less scary
than he did
because to the best of my knowledge
in Fishersgate
they don't have cannibal stories -
just cannabis ones.

2010

SHED FIRE
Inspired by a headline on the billboard for our local newspaper...

A perfect English pageantry:
an act so gloriously mundane
New neighbours put up eight foot fence
So strangers now will thus remain
As English as our small town press
who'd like so much to dish the dirt
but headline uneventfulness:
'Local shed fire. No-one hurt.'

A cod war veteran complains
about some kids skateboarding by
The Daily Mail sells very well
And he and it see eye to eye
The homeless sleep under the pier
But most round here don't seem to care
That's city life, another's news.
Shed fire, though. Police aware.

The poster shouts it, black and white
A headline story, that's for sure
And there's a pull out TV guide
For folk who rarely ask for more
And two, more lively than the rest,
Are chatting in the autumn sun.
Not in their back yard, thank god,
But shed fire. Little damage done.

2004

SLOUGH
In response to Betjeman's calumny on the place I shall forever know as The Berkshire Riviera...

Come tourists all, and flock to Slough
as many as the streets allow
By bus, or train - no matter how -
Come, very soon!

And lift forever the sad curse
once laid in dull, sarcastic verse
by one whose poetry is worse
than Mills and Boon!

Sir John - oh, what a sense of farce!
A poet of the teacup class
obsessed with railways, and stained glass
and twisted bough

and thus impervious to the call
of the post-war suburban sprawl
of Harlow, Basildon and all
and glorious Slough!

Oh Slough! Harbinger of my dreams!
Home of a thousand training schemes
and theme pubs, patronised by streams
of tetchy men

with blow-dried hair and blow-dried brain
diplomas in inflicting pain
and ne'er a thought for Larkin, Raine
and Betjeman!

A thousand jewellers' shops contend
The kitchen unit is your friend
Designer labels set the trend
with a blank stare

Attila The Stockbroker

And now - the latest, brightest star -
a brand new ten screen cinema!
The folk will come from near and far
to worship there!

Oh self-made, independent town!
The jewel in Margaret's southern crown!
No more will poets put you down
with mocking voice!

Come tourists all, and flock to Slough
as Milton Friedman takes a bow
This town is fit for heroes now -
Come, and rejoice!

1988

Three Martian Love Poems

Martianism was a poetic 'school' invented by in the 80s by Craig Raine, in which the poet looked at the world through the eyes of a visitor from Mars and described everyday human interactions in a strange way. It, erm, lent itself to parody.

TO SLOUGH AND SANITY

Far from our city haunts,
besieged on all sides,
we stumble apprehensively
through a minefield of cowpats.
The cloying earth
sucks greedily at your high heels
and you surrender reluctantly
to the ditch's embrace.
Crouching to your aid, I suddenly see before me
all of Flanders in 1916 –
trench, barbed wire, stinging nettles,
broken glass, maggots…
the stench of death.
As my outstretched arm levers you upright
you suggest that I may be guilty of pretentiousness
and ill-timed remarks
and as I purse my lips in reply
the enemy come over the top!
Huge, lumbering tanks,
Lowing deeply:
an armoury of udders –
bitter mammaries indeed!
With a yell, I sound the alarm
and we beat a disorderly retreat
to Slough, and sanity.

1988

WORTHING

On the beach at Worthing
the lugworm casts
by the sewage outfall
look like dirty shepherds' pie.
We walk the shingle
hand in hand
and the crabs on the nearby groyne
remind me of more intimate times.
Your hand resembles a limp flounder.
I squeeze it dispassionately.
The seaweed smells like a dirty toilet.
Refreshed, we return for dinner.

1989

DUSTBIN POEM

Today I took out the rubbish
and thought of you.
At the bottom of my dustbin
the maggots wriggled round and round
like planes circling over Heathrow Airport.
Now and then two larval aviators collided
in the crowded, circular, putrescent grooves of metal
and I thought yes, this is us –
not even ships that pass in the night
but maggots wriggling in predetermined circles
in the putrescent dustbin
of the enterprise culture.

1990

NEW BRIGHTON

For years I'd been aware that my home town had an allegedly more recent namesake, nestling on the tip of the Wirral Peninsular. So during a series of gigs in the Northwest I went on a pilgrimage and afterwards wrote a poem of comparison...

No supercilious yuppie hordes
No rip-off absentee landlords
No crap stude chains to ruin your pub
No overpriced, pretentious grub
No begging crusties hooked on smack
No London dealers pushing crack
No narrow streets clogged up with cars
No endless naff expresso bars
No pissed up blokes who fight and sing
No beer, no life, no...anything!
There IS a fort. Says 'Open'. But
The gates are resolutely shut.
New Brighton. That's a good idea -
But it's not going to happen here.

2006

STORNOWAY

My parents honeymooned on the Isle of Harris, and Mum always wanted to return there one day. I finally took her one summer, with hopes of some music and fishing thrown in. It is accessed via the other half of the island, Lewis, and its capital, Stornoway. The ferry pulled in on a Sunday.

Why did we come to Stornoway?
I do not know. I cannot say.
The sea is oil. The sky is grey.
It rains and rains and rains all day.
No pollack bite. No fiddles play.
Just techno in a sad café
A spotty waitress with a tray
And dull religion to obey.
I wish I was in Whitley Bay
Up to my neck in Beaujolais
Or prodding General Pinochet
With an extremely sharp epee
Or modelling my knob in clay
While watching Galataseray
Or somewhere different, anyway –
Because this place is quite manqué
And I do not intend to stay.
Oh dirty, ugly Stornoway….
Devoid of bass and sole and ray
And cod, skate, place and mullet grey
I came to fish, hear music play.
It's crap! I'm going to go away!

1994

HARROGATE

At length expelled from Bradford Bus
For the first time in Harrogate
I vowed I would not make a Fuss
Nor get Drunk, nor Expectorate

For Such Behaviour would not fit
this Rest Home for the Middle Classes
(I saw a quaint Optician's. It
Dispensed 'Eye-Wear': yes, that means Glasses.)

Blue Rinse was everywhere, and Tea.
And under every Lady's Pillow
In this Hub of Complacency
The Fuhrer's Photo. Hail Portillo!

But then I found the Hostelry
In which the Poet was to read.
Oh Pain! Oh Sad Grotesquerie!
What Contrast was there here, indeed…

A Toilet in the midst of Taste.
A Foetid Cuckoo in the Nest.
The Landlord harassed, and in Haste.
The Beer just Piss. I should have guessed.

He wasn't sure that I would come,
He said. Hence, no Publicity.
The Drinkers in this Awful Dive
wanted a Disco. They got me.

But, as you know, I do not shrink
From Challenges, and took them on.
I made most of the Punters think.
The rest played Pool, their braincells gone.

Heart On My Sleeve

Then, in the middle of my Set,
Some started up a Football Game.
I love Football in Poetry – yet
Combined this way, it was a shame.

Still, they were Friendly Folk enough.
I took my fee, as well I ought,
And even sold some tapes and stuff.
Then trundled off. My final thought

On Harrogate: Well, it looks nice.
Though living here must surely bore yer.
And, Poets All, take my Advice:
Stay well clear of the Honest Lawyer!

1996

BRAINTREE

After all the (rightful) fuss about genetically modified food, here's my first genetically modified poem...

On balance, I think,
I'm opposed to genetic modification.
However, this does seem
a very good idea.
Millions would benefit.
After several good harvests
tabloids would fold
television become an underground cult
celebrity an obsolete concept -
spectators, participants.
But we would need so many....
Could your Essex soil sustain such forests?
For we would need forests, huge forests
in this dumbed-down land of ours.
No, sorry, Essex:
we'd have to plant over the border -
Cambridgeshire, perhaps -
and use your natural resources,
your legions of terse, musclebound,
unemployed nightclub bouncers
to guard the precious forests
from Murdoch's scab geneticists
employed, as they surely would be,
to infiltrate late at night
and inject the moron gene back
into the growing fruit.
A grandiose scheme.
A bit ambitious, perhaps.
But it does seem
a wonderful idea.
Let's start off small
and plant just one
in precisely the place in all England
where it is needed the most.
I know.

Heart On My Sleeve

I used to live there.

We'll set its roots deep
in Harlow town centre
between the Jean Harlow pub,
the disco
and the kebabery
to cast its awesome shadow of wisdom
over testosterone and lager
giving up its heavy, undulating, grey, veiny fruit
to the weekend combatants
so that each and every one
wakes next morning
to The Guardian, Vivaldi and Radio Four.
And The Clash of course.

News would spread fast.
Soon Basildon would have one.
The Lakeside Centre in Thurrock
would sustain a small plantation.
Every shopping mall in England
would put in an order
and soon each would boast one
next to the tasteless water feature.
And then....
Export.
To France?
Home of Sartre and Camus?
I'm sure there would be objections.
A ban, whatever the EU position.
Non! Danger of infection!
Coals to Newcastle!
But hang on, messieurs-dames:
you have Le Pen,
National Front town councils
and beer so foul
even John Smith's pales in comparison.

Therefore:
Objection overruled!

From Essex to the world.
The best thing since The Newtown Neurotics,
Wat Tyler and Ian Dury.
The ultimate genetic modification!
Braintree.

2008

FOYER BAR
(Harlow, 1982)

Living in a brave new town
Things can often get you down
Not much to say, not much to do
Existence gets on top of you
And some folk say well why not go
And meet a girl in a disco
But I don't want to walk that far
So I go to the foyer bar

We go there and we sit together
Uniform is jeans and leather
And we sit and drink and doze
And we sit and drink and pose
Everything we say is cool
Big fish in a little pool
Yes, if you want to be a star
You'll make it in the foyer bar!

SEALAND
Commissioned by Radio 4's 'The Last Word'.

In the age of the passive consumer
Where the TV and sofa hold sway
Raise a glass to those brave noncomformists
Who say 'sod that!' and go their own way.
One such fellow was Prince Roy of Sealand.
A country out in the North Sea.
I say 'country' – more guano-strewn platform.
But for him, it was the place to be.

On Roughs Tower, a small fort just off Harwich,
Left to rot at the end of the war
Roy started his own pirate radio
To the shock of the big wigs onshore
At the height of the flower power era
This project seemed quite a strange call
Cos his hero was old Frank Sinatra
And he didn't like pop stuff at all….

He tired of the radio station –
He needed a much bigger throne
So decided to start his own country
As a birthday gift for his wife, Joan.
Thus she became Princess of Sealand –
But the government was not impressed
They sank all the other forts out there
And told Prince and Princess: 'You're next!'

But their fort was outside jurisdiction –
International waters, you see
And the courts ruled in Roy Bates' favour
Which meant his dear Sealand was free!
He made passports, and stamps, and a coinage
And he started a football team too
They played Alderney and the Aland Islands. *
(I don't know quite where they are. Do you?)

Heart On My Sleeve

As an old International Brigader
Of large build and stentorian tone
He defended his country with gusto
When usurpers came after his throne
With petrol bombs, bullets and insults
He dealt with invaders with ease
Then locked them all up in his jail.
Not a man that you'd want to displease.

He named son Prince Michael as Regent
When too frail to rule all on his own
And he died on the ninth of October
In a Leigh on Sea old people's home
'Old or young I may die' he once told us
In an interview some years ago
'But I know that I'll not die of boredom!'
And you didn't, Prince Roy. Way to go.

2009

LITTLE ENGLAND

ASYLUM-SEEKING DALEKS

They claim their planet's dying:
that soon it's going to blow
And so they're coming here - they say
they've nowhere else to go
With their strange computer voices
and their one eye on a pole
They're moving in next door and then
they're signing on the dole...

Asylum-seeking Daleks
are landing here at noon!
Why can't we simply send them back
or stick them on the moon?
It says here in the Daily Mail
they're coming here to stay -
The Loony Lefties let them in!
The middle class will pay...

They say that they're not terrorists:
That doesn't wash with me!
The last time I saw one I hid
Weeks behind the settee...
Good Lord - they're pink. With purple bumps!
There's photos of them here!
Not just extra-terrestial...
The bloody things are queer!

Heart On My Sleeve

Yes! Homosexual Daleks
And they're sponging off the State!
With huge Arts Council grants
to teach delinquents how to skate!
It's all here in the paper -
I'd better tell the wife!
For soon they will EXTERMINATE
Our British way of life...

This satire on crass ignorance
and tabloid-fostered fear
Is at an end. Now let me give
One message, loud and clear.
Golf course, shop floor or BNP:
Smash bigotry and hate!
Asylum seekers - welcome here.
You racists: emigrate!

2005

TAKE BACK CONTROL
(For Ronnie Chambers in Hartlepool)

You tell me how you've suffered since the closure.
I see the pain and sadness in your eyes.
I feel your anger at our country's leaders
Who offer only platitudes and lies.
At gigs I hear so many of these stories.
All different, but the message is the same.
You're sick to death of scheming politicians.
No longer going to play their poxy game.

The referendum was your chance. You took it.
They told you we'd be taking back control.
Control of jobs and factories and borders:
A revolution wrapped up in a poll.
The EU is a massive corporate bully.
Cheap labour and big profits at its core.
I understand why you voted for Brexit:
One chance to strike a blow in the class war.

But it wasn't the EU who shut your pit down
And sent Met thugs rampaging through your street.
It didn't close your hospitals and workshops
Smash down your union to brave defeat.
No EU diktat caused the housing crisis
The poll tax, bedroom tax or zero hours.
No, all of these were brought in by the Tories -
And soon those bastards will have brand new powers.

So let's take back control with strong trade unions
And let's take back control and organise
Take back control of pub and school and workplace
And counter all the endless media lies.
Take back control as we all stand together
No scapegoating and no divide and rule.
The future is unwritten, and it's daunting.
Please don't let Brexit take you for a fool.

2016

OPINION FARM

Welcome to Opinion Farm.
Cummings wants you to self harm
To promote the stocks and shares
Of a group of billionaires.
They need Britain to go under
So they can exploit and plunder
But they cloak their heartless blag
In a massive Union flag.
They have headlines, broadcasts, memes.
All are backed by hedge fund schemes.
When they say 'take back control'
They mean 'stick you on the dole.'
When it's 'freedom with no deal'
They mean 'break you on the wheel'.
They're not patriots. Don't be fooled
If you would be fairly ruled.

2020

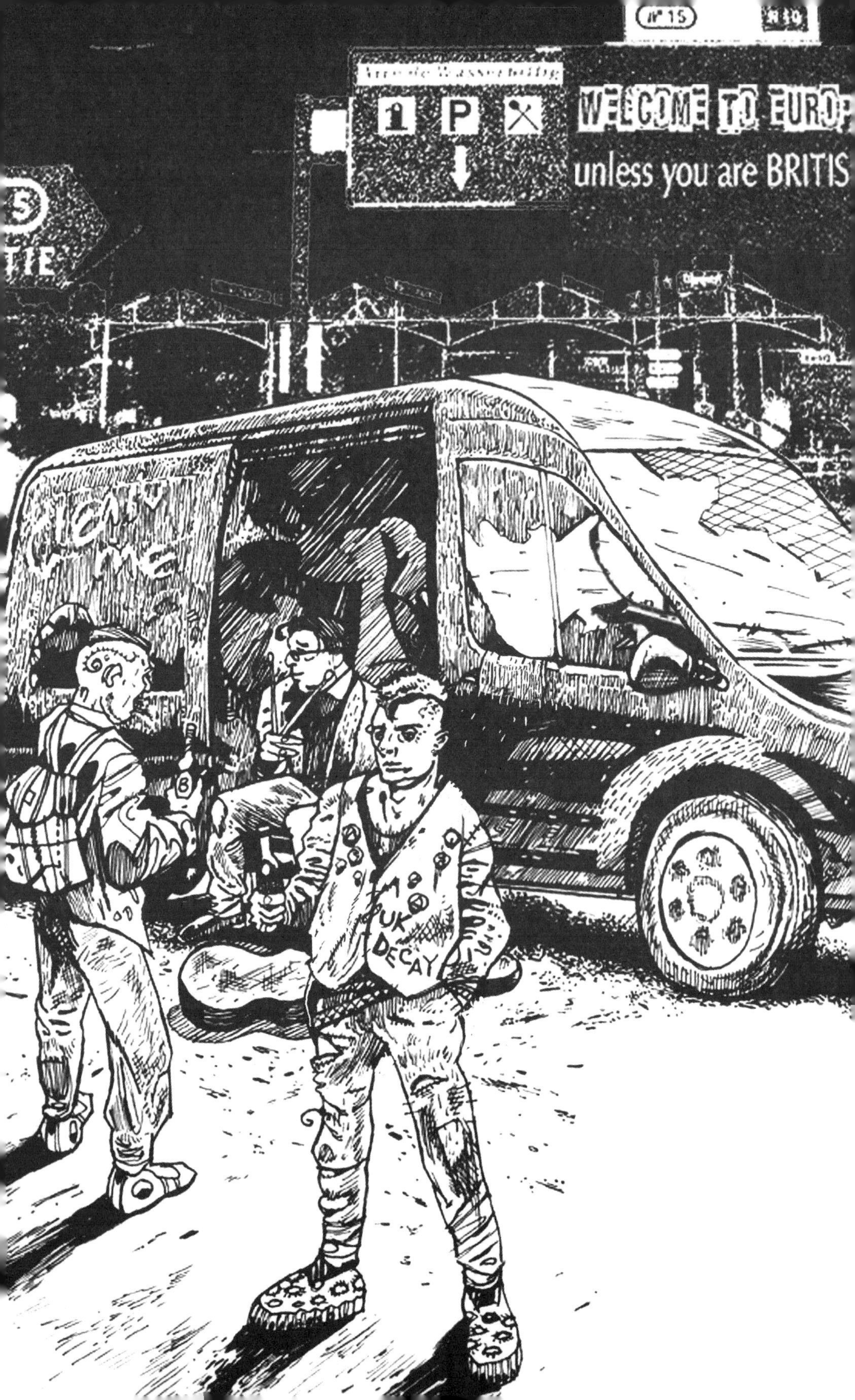
WELCOME TO EUROP
unless you are BRITIS
UK DECAY

ROCK 'N' ROLL BREXIT
(Written on the ferry home, Oct 10 2016)

I've just toured with my band Barnstormer
from Dunkirk to Lucerne and back
through France, Belgium, Germany and Switzerland
without showing a passport once.
Yes, non-EU Switzerland too –
a little bridge, an empty hut.
In my punk rock youth
I remember
how musicians had to carry carnets
for our instruments
when we crossed the Channel -
everything down to the last spare string
painstakingly listed on a pointless green form
checked and stamped at every border
after standing with the truckers in endless queues.
I remember the invasive French customs
- douane, not moeurs -
whose cretinously predictable searches
for non-existent drugs
took the edge off many an otherwise enjoyable tour.
Search the big posh cars
driven by the suits,
I'd always say
after these unimaginative custodians
had finished their fruitless checks:
no-one imports half a ton of heroin
dressed like we are
driving a scruffy transit van
with 'CLEAN ME'
written in the dirt on one side
'WE HATE CRYSTAL PALACE'
on the other
a large knob and testicles
adorning the back
and empty beer bottles
rolling around on the floor.

Are we going to have to go through all this again?
Just because Rupert Murdoch
was pissed off by the fact
that no one in Brussels
took a blind bit of notice of him?
Lord give me strength!

Only joking, of course.
Brexit was an informed decision
taken by the British people
after serious consideration
of the established facts
presented intelligently
and objectively
by the rigorous guardians
of the Fourth Estate.
And anyone who suggests anything else
is patronising and supercilious.
So if in a few years time
a British number plate for a band touring Europe
becomes the equivalent of a plague signal on a door
in medieval times
and I am once again obliged to fill in ridiculous forms
and perhaps even at my advanced age
stand naked in a room
with a gloved finger up my arse
and my foreskin peeled back
as I once did in Calais in the Eighties
I shall hold myself proudly to attention
and celebrate the fact
that I am British
and we have
Taken
Back
Control.

2016

EVERY TIME I EAT VEGETABLES…

No agony, no ecstacy, no pleasure and no pain –
So exquisitely uninteresting you drive your wife insane
The TV is your oracle, the newspapers your guide
And your shiny little vehicle is your passion and your pride
You've done the same thing every day for nigh on twenty years
And in your ludicrous routines you hide your worthless fears
On the blandest boat in Boredom you are captain of the crew
And every time I eat vegetables it makes me think of you.

You died the day that you were born and now you sit and rot –
A three piece suited dinsoaur in the pond that time forgot
Your image is respectable, there's nothing underneath
And the whole thing is as surely false as nine tenths of your teeth
Your views are carbon copies of the rubbish that you read
And you swallow every morsel Rupert Murdoch seeks to feed
You go to bed at ten because you've nothing else to do
And every time I eat vegetables it makes me think of you.

You're a cabbage in a pickle and your brain has sprung a leek
So lettuce keep our distance 'cos I vomit when you speak
I'll always do a runner so I'm going where you've bean
'Cos to see you chills my marrow and turns my tomatoes green
You're an eighteen carrot cretin with a dandelion whine –
So stick to your herbaceous border and I'll stick to mine
And although this verse is corny, it's amaizing but it's true
That every time I eat vegetables it makes me think of you!

1980

UK GIN DEPENDENCE PARTY

We're not fascists, are we, dear?
Bring that bottle over here.
Now. Where was I? Enoch Powell.
Damn this irritable bowel!
Do you play goff? Come down the club.
Just a snifter, lovely grub...
What, no blazer? Borrow mine.
Chin chin. Maggie, '79!

Now. Where was I? Nigel Farage.
Dear! More bottles in the garage.
Really don't want to disparage
But he should pronounce it 'Farridge'.
Agincourt and Waterloo
Showed those Frenchies what to do.
Entente Cordiale - bloody shame.
Wonder how he got that name?

Now. Where was I? Edward Heath.
Awful man with awful teeth.
He's the one who started this -
Led us into the abyss.
It would have been so much easier
To have teamed up with Rhodesia.
Bloody Poles. This gin is strong...
Oh, it's vodka. Got that wrong!

Now, where was I? Fascists? No.
I fought them, I'll have you know.
Well, I nearly did – too young.
Something's happening to my tongue!
Bloody Poles. I need a kip.
Do have one more. Just a nip...
Upstairs, ere my senses fail.
Eileen, where's the Daily Mail?

Heart On My Sleeve

One last parting shot, young man:
Country's going down the pan.
Anyone with half a brain
Is selling up and orf to Spain.
Part of that's in Europe, true -
But not the bit we're going to.
Bloody Poles. My poor old head...
See yourself out. Orf to bed!

2008

POISON PENSIONER

I've tried to work it out but I just can't see
How a cretin like you is related to me
You've just one brain cell and that one's a mess
Parroting rubbish from the Daily Express
No, not the Sun: you'd say that was a 'rag'
Delusions of grandeur from a jumped up hag
But don't get ideas: you're as thick as a shoe
Poison pensioner - this poem's for you

I've had it up to here and I'm cutting up rough
Distant relative? Not distant enough!
Ever thought of space travel, prejudiced cow?
I'd suggest Uranus but you're up there right now
You've a monochrome vision of a world that's dead
A million Reader's Digests inside your head
I'd like to put vomit in your cheese fondue
Poison pensioner – this poem's for you

You worked all your life in the public sector
And all you ever did was whine and hector
Moan about the people who fought your cause
Cheer for the Tories and their union laws
You were born in a council house, you clueless bitch
But you side with the Right and you vote with the rich
Bowing and scraping to the privileged few
Poison pensioner - this poem's for you

Heart On My Sleeve

You've a medal for meddling, that's for sure
If this was my house then I'd show you the door
But my mum needs help and you're here to see her
So I sit and listen to your verbal gonorrhea
Right now I wish I was in her head
'Cos Mum won't remember a word you've said
Your compassionate act just got a bad review
Poison pensioner - this poem's for you

Bossy yet servile, some combination!
Paralysed spine of a lickspittle nation
Could have been a builder, ended up a tool
Lifelong victim of divide and rule
You're a Ragged Trousered Philanthropist
Who wasn't even waiting for the boat you've missed
You're a turkey voting for Christmas too
Poison pensioner - this poem's for you

2003

USE OF ENGLISH

The phrase 'politically correct'
Is not at all what you'd expect.
But how has it been hijacked so?
I'm going to tell you, 'cos I know.

You'd think it should mean kind and smart
Radical and stout of heart
A way of living decently.
Well, so it did, till recently.

And then some cringing, nerdy divs
Sweaty, misogynistic spivs
Sad, halitosis-ridden hacks
All wearing lager-stained old macs
With spots and pustules and split ends
And absolutely zero friends
(Yes, living, breathing running sores:
The right wing press's abject whores)
Were all told, by their corporate chiefs
To rubbish decent folks' beliefs
To label with the phrase 'P.C'
All that makes sense to you and me
And write off our progressive past.
Their articles came thick and fast
The editors gladly received them
And loads of idiots believed them.

You'll find that most who use the term
Will only do so to affirm
Sad, bigoted, outdated views
They've swallowed via the Murdoch news.

2000

AN 'IN/OUT REFERENDUM ON EUROPE' IS A GEOGRAPHICAL NON-STARTER, CAMERON, YOU DICKHEAD!

This one was a bit prophetic…

There are six continents.
Asia, America, Antarctica, Australia, Africa and Europe.
The UK isn't in any of the other five, is it, Cameron?
Is it, UK Gin Dependence Party?
Is it, Daily Express, Sun, Daily Mail reading amoeba heads?
Did you DO geography at school?
Inger-land, Blighty, The Old Country, whatever, is in EUROPE.
We - all of us – are indisputably, implacably EUROPEAN!

We are. And there is absolutely nothing you can do about it.
The only kind of relationship the UK has with Europe is the kind you have with that lager-filled beer gut of yours, or your gin and tonic habit, or your gout, or the nasty disease you caught from your butler, or if you're a true member of the aristocracy, someone in your close family. We are as much a part of Europe as they are a part of you. You might not like it... but we are.

WE ARE JOINED TO EUROPE.
Ok, there is a bit of sea in the way,
but underneath that bit of sea there isn't some kind of SURREAL GAP,
there is a land mass, and that land mass is EUROPE.
WE ARE JOINED TO IT!

That's right. One day you might develop a functioning braincell, and then you will realize that this country is as much a part of Europe as France, Liechtenstein or any of those other strange places where the inhabitants speak a language which you don't understand!
We are European.
Like every other country in Europe.
One among many.
Not special.
Got it?

The only way we are special is that we are the only country in Europe apart from France where 90% of the population can't speak a foreign language!

Ah, you'll say, you're not talking about the physical geography of Europe, you're talking about the EU. I'm not actually very keen on the EU, since I am for a European Union of the people. I am against a Europe dominated by slimy pinstriped capitalist scum. But then, I'm against a world dominated by slimy capitalist scum and, sadly, it most certainly is right now. So, in the same way that the UK isn't a special case in Europe, Europe isn't a special case in the world.

On that basis I LOVE the EU and ADORE the Euro.
Why? Because they wind up xenophobic, Little Englander, moronic tabloid newspaper reading, 'isn't it hot' complaining, 'isn't it cold' complaining, barathea blazer wearing, delusions of 'Ingerlish' grandeur suffering, 'PC' as a term of abuse employing IDIOTS! Ban the pound! Fill in the English Channel! Superglue the UK to France, right in the middle of the garlic growing region – NOW!

And no, I don't want a referendum.

2013

THERE'S A MAN DOWN OUR ROAD WHO'S A NAZI
A while ago, the entire BNP membership list was released online. Names, addresses and all. I had a look...

There's a man down our road who's a Nazi!
He's there on the list, that's for sure
His hobbies are bowls and line dancing
And he lives at 204...
Well, I must say that he looks quite normal
And his wife makes a nice cup of tea
There's a man down our road who's a Nazi!
I'm glad he's not next door to me...

He's bald, but, no, he's not a skinhead
He wears Hush Puppies, not those big boots
His dog's a shitsu, not a pitbull
And he doesn't goose step, he - commutes!
It's a Rotary Club badge, I'm certain
That little one on his lapel
There's a man down our road who's a Nazi!
Goes to show that you never can tell...

I bet that his wife is embarrassed
And she wishes that nobody knew
Now they're calling her 'Eva' - that's horrid!
Been expelled from the W.I. too...
Do they really? What, NOTHING but Wagner?
AND so loud that the neighbours complain?
There's a man down our road who's a Nazi!
And there's talk of a local campaign!

Yes, I know you work at the newsagents.
What has that got to do with this tale?
You're right! It's the proof. Yes, we've got him.
Life subscription to the Daily Mail......
Who, of course, said 'Hooray for the Blackshirts!'
Now it all makes complete sense to me.
There's a man down our road who's a Nazi!
He's as Nazi as Nazi can be!

2008

THOUGHTS ON THE 'MARCH FOR ENGLAND', BRIGHTON 27/4/2014

For a number of years, around the time of St George's Day, a pathetic gaggle of right-wing nutters travelling from all over the country attempted with a spectacular lack of success to march through Brighton, rightly seeing us as a symbol of tolerance and multiculturalism and loathing us for it. White, working class and angry – angry with the wrong people.

Let's march for England 'gainst a common foe –
The greedy, heartless, ignorant and cruel.
Not as Ragged Trousered Philanthropists
Conned by the clichés of divide and rule.

We've food banks now. Kids go hungry to school.
No cause for pride, just deep, heartbroken shame.
And yet, somehow, not Cameron's banker friends
But we, radical Brighton, are to blame!

So fight the power, don't pick a fight with us.
Defend all those who weep and starve and parch.
When we stand for our rights in union, Jack,
Then England will be truly on the march!

XENOPHOBIA

At the time I thought this was satire. I didn't realise that in 2020 it would become official government policy post Brexit.

THE DUTCH the Dutch they're much too much we're gonna kick them in the crutch flick bogies at the slimy frogs and trip them up with their own clogs we'll twist their ears and break their glasses stick their tulips up their arses foul their windmills with our bowels and vomit into their canals THE DANES the Danes we'll bash their brains and wire their willies to the mains boycott their bacon and their prawns and go and piss over their lawns the scabby Scandinavian scum got scrotal scabies of the bum they live on fish-heads and weak tea their lager tastes like canine pee THE SWISS the Swiss they stink of piss no race more tedious than this with cuckoo clocks and huge amounts of money in their bank accounts they may be rich but we don't care we'll shave off all their pubic hair and make them live in Belgium - that's the right place for the boring prats THE FRENCH the French they smell like tench we'll chase them all into a trench get loads of garlic on our breath and suffocate them all to death we don't like onions snails or Proust so smeg off frogs we rule the roost you may be existentialists but we're dead hard and we get pissed the CZECHS the Czechs they're scared of sex they've all got crabs and skinny necks their cars are shit their beer's too strong we're not gonna stay there for long there's absolutely zilch to do there's no Black Label and no glue so we'll just wreck the place and go and leave them to their queues and snow the FINNS the Finns live out of tins they all look like the Cocteau Twins their scenery's not very nice 'cos most of it's a mass of ice so don't go there it's much too chilly you'll end up with a frozen willy it's a godforsaken hole obscenely close to the North Pole THE KRAUTS the Krauts they think they're louts but I've seen nastier Brussels sprouts they strut around like football yobs but they're all talk and cheesy knobs they live on pickled vegetation what a fucking stupid nation all their nipples are bright green the strangest folk I've ever seen THE SWEDES the Swedes they're fucking weeds and all their cities look like Leeds they walk around with plastic bags and noses stuck in porno mags they live on fish just like the Danes but they've got even smaller brains their language sounds like double Dutch their land smells like a llama's crutch THE GREEKS the Greeks we'll slap their cheeks and lock them up in bogs for weeks puke in their restaurants and bars and write rude slogans on their cars we'll get a load of herpes scabs and stick 'em all in their kebabs and write a note IN PUKE to say 'CLUB 18-30 RULE OK!!' THE POLES the Poles eat toilet rolls their underpants are full of holes they have to queue over an hour to get a mouldy cauliflower they whine and whinge and gripe and moan and play the hairy pink trombone they're always wanking in the loo there's fuck all else for them to do THE YANKS the Yanks... duh... many thanks for bringing in your bombs and tanks and crossing many a foreign border to bolster up the New World Order you're foreigners but you're alright 'cos you speak English and you fight or so it tells me in the Sun...
COR! BEING A MORON IS SUCH FUN!

1989

LANGUAGE BARRIER

A man was beaten to death in August 1992 at a burger stall in Kingston-on-Thames in 1992 apparently because, though English, he was speaking in French to his female companions...

'Oi, you!
Whaddya talking foreign for?
You're English like us, aintcha?
So whaddya talking foreign for?
Nice birds though, ya done alright there, mate
But watcha talking like that for?
Oh, they don't speak English, don't they?
Well, whyya bothering with them Froggie slags then?
Talking never did any good anyway – give us 'em over 'ere,
they can talk to our meat, that's Esperanto, innit?
Watcha sayin to em? Oi, cunt, watcha sayin to 'em?
Talkin bahrt us, are ya?
Fuckin wanker
Bet ya think yer really clever-clever, dontcha,
talkin foreign so we can't understand ya
trying to impress those birds with yer fancy lingo –
fucking university wanker
Hey, you lot, shall we TALK to 'im, eh?
Poncy cunt – let's teach him a REAL lesson, eh?
Oh, not so mouthy now, are we, wanker?
Well, it's too late – we're gonna kick some good British sense into
yer, aren't we, lads?
No use begging now, ya student tosser!'

And the boots went in
the fists went in
and he went down
the boots went in again
the fists went in again
and the lights went out on a life
destroyed in a blind moment of hatred
by the psychopathic flotsam of Thatcherism's own –
and let's have no excuses,
no bullshit sociology,
no talk of deprivation, of mitigating circumstances –
Kingston-on-Thames?

Heart On My Sleeve

No, these were just mean-spirited scum,
celebrating the values of the last thirteen years –
the values of crass ignorance
selfishness
violence
and of course
'pride in being British'.
Was it for this, the 1944 Education Act?

People are murdered every day, of course
often for even more unbelievably banal reasons
so why this poem?
Simply that I remember
a visit to a pub
my own bilingual conversation
(it's a skill, you learn it, like medicine or carpentry –
a skill that most Europeans take for granted)
and the broken beer glass
and the contorted face of the thug
when I replied to his insult in his own tongue.
For me it ended differently
but when I saw that story in the paper
a shiver ran down my spine
I remembered that evening in the pub
and the impotent anger swelled uncontrollably in my guts.

One final thought.
I bet THIS senseless murder
didn't make the tabloid headlines:
After all,
The Paper That Supports Our Boys
wouldn't want to alienate its readership,
would it?

1992

KEEPING UP APPEARANCES
For all those touched by the Grenfell Tower massacre – still seeking justice three years on

'The clue's in the name. Royal Borough.
We serve Knightsbridge, not Latimer Road.
We're here for our quality voters
With a moneyed and tasteful postcode.
We tolerate you since we have to
And we hope that you'll soon move elsewhere.
Until then we'll do our legal duty.
If you cause any problems – beware!

Your flats are all crumbling eyesores.
Your neighbours are your social betters.
They paid millions to live in this area -
Some are next door to scroungers and debtors.
So it's time to refurbish your building.
Not with fire doors, sprinklers and care
But with cladding to make it look nicer
So the rich can pretend you're not there.

It's unsafe, you complain. That's just rubbish.
We've been running it that way for years.
Just be grateful you're housed in this borough
And make sure that you're not in arrears!
You've new skins on your homes. They look lovely.
Regulations and standards are met.
All done legally and within budget
So get on with your lives and don't fret.'

Those new skins caused a ghastly inferno.
But that council is still in control
Though some should be charged with manslaughter
And the rest all relieved of their role.
Now the people cry 'Justice for Grenfell!'
In the name of those folk left alone
In a world where appearances mattered
More than flesh, skin, hair, muscle and bone.

2017

FURTHER AFIELD

MOUNTAINEERING IN BELGIUM

In the mountains of Belgium,
just outside Ghent,
I take your arm
and, apprehensively,
we begin our descent.
On chariots of wire, we wander
the high walled peaks
of this consumer paradise
and I marvel
at the natural beauty
and fertility
of a Flemish valley.
Suddenly the checkout lady,
noting my vacant stare,
enquires if I need the toilet,
curses in a guttural burp,
and throws us onto the street.
Mountaineering in Belgium
is not as simple
as it looks.

1989

CANADA SURPRISE

I am playing at a plush, antiseptic businessman's dinner and dance establishment called the Norwood Hotel: it's my first gig in Winnipeg and it seems completely self-evident that no-one round here has the faintest idea what Attila the Stockbroker is. The gig has been organized at very short notice by the Winnipeg Folk Festival: as far as I can tell the publicity consists of a box ad in the hotel restaurant menu and a couple of leaflets shoved between the Grateful Dead albums in the local second-hand record store. There is a two-dollar admission charge, waived for anyone staying at or entertaining in the hotel.

The majority of the audience consists of businessmen: corporate males, each with one of those little cardboard identification badges which middle-aged executives wear in lieu of personalities when they go to business functions in hotels. They are all rather drunk, and obviously under the impression that Attila the Stockbroker is some kind of country and western act.

There's a smatter of Folk Club regulars, mostly Woodstock survivors and Arran sweater victims, and, to my pleasure and surprise, a group of ten or so who look like punks and show every sign of interest – in fact all of them come up to me individually during the course of the evening and ask me why the hell I'm playing at a country and western club instead of the local anarcho-veggie commune, and will I come and play for them there after I've been booed off?

At the appointed hour I take the stage. Directly in front of me, and seemingly oblivious to my presence, four gentlemen of the wrist talk corporate gunk – their lapel badges indicating an umbilical allegiance to a local computer firm. Summoning up all my considerable energy reserves, I launch into an extra loud, extra fast version of 'Libyan Students From Hell' and await the onslaught.

An hour and a half and three encores later, I leave the stage – very worried.

1990

AUSTRALIAN DECOMPOSITION

I'm not much one for snapshots, though the world is now my oyster
I chronicle my wanderings in poem and in song
But when I went Down Under, I brought along my camera
To chronicle the wildlife, that rich and teeming throng
On my first few days in Oz I wasn't sure that they existed
Those strange exotic species they mostly run away
But on the way to Melbourne, the truth became apparent:
If you want to see some animals, take the motorway!

There are wallabies and wombats, there are possums, birds and lizards
And kangaroos of all sorts, yes even a big red
And all these different creatures have one special thing in common -
Yes, each of them is stinkingly, spectacularly dead.

There are lots of flies in Aussie: now I know where they all come from
For there were loads of maggots in the creatures that I saw
Yes, every little corpsie was a blowfly kindergarten –
More wrigglers and more squirmers than I've ever seen before
Now I've made my contribution to Australian natural history
And it's in that country's honour that I decomposed this song
But one word of advice to any wild death photographer –
Stay inside the car because the bastards don't half pong!

And with a squelch, another hapless kanga rues the day
That the Government of Victoria built that brand new motorway...

1991

PUNK NIGHT AT THE DUCK'S NUTS

It's a Wednesday night
in Newcastle, New South Wales.
There's a pub right next to our hotel
called 'The Duck's Nuts.'
(To emphasise the point,
next to the entrance
there's a large mural of a duck on a surfboard
with his testicles hanging out.
Yes, I know ducks don't have nuts.
But this one has.
I can see them.)

I can't believe it.
'Hey, Mick' I say,
I can't believe it!
'There's a pub right next to our hotel
called 'The Duck's Nuts!'
And look at this mural!'
Mick's not really surprised at all.
He explains that in Australian
to say something is 'the duck's nuts'
means you think it's really, really good.
That figures, I guess.
In England, if we think something's really, really good
we say it's 'the dog's bollocks' -
at least my friends and I do.
I doubt if the Queen does.
Nevertheless, I am still surprised
because to the best of my knowledge
we don't have any pubs in England called 'The Dog's Bollocks'
nor any pub signs which feature dogs' testicles
- though it's true that we do have a beer of that name.
Typical English understatement,
I suppose.

Anyway, Mick and I have just done a gig
at Newcastle University

supporting a very famous Aussie band called the Whitlams
who sound like Supertramp on Mogadon.
We've escaped
it's past midnight
and a beer or two at The Duck's Nuts
seems like a very good idea.

But there's no Dog's Bollocks at the Duck's Nuts -
in fact, nothing even remotely drinkable
for a real ale fan like myself -
and the lager I am handed is unspeakable:
the hamster's bladder contents and then some.
There is a punk band playing in the corner.
The guitarist has spiky hair and a broken hand.
They are playing Green Day covers very loudly
and after the Whitlams, they sound absolutely bloody fantastic to me.
There are about twenty people in the pub
all of whom are over sixty
all of whom are very pissed.
To be the youngest person at a gig
isn't something that happens to me much these days -
but it hardly seems to matter.

The audience
- if one can call them an audience -
is staring at the band.
They obviously don't think they are the duck's nuts
or the dog's bollocks
or even the lemming's gonads
because they don't applaud
at the end of the songs
they just drink, stare into space
and get even more pissed
- which is very pissed indeed.

We applaud.
We're musicians.
We sympathise.
And anyway I think they're pretty good

Attila The Stockbroker

(for a Green Day covers band...)

Suddenly they stop playing
and announce they're having a break.
A break?
It's one o'clock in the morning
and they're stopping for a break?
Yes, they've got to do two more sets -
in the middle of the night
to twenty semi-comatose pensioners
who by now are completely oblivious to their surroundings.

I think of the worst gigs I have ever done.
There is no contest.
I have seen Hell.

Jean Paul Sartre wasn't specific enough.
Hell is not other people.
Hell is three sets
between midnight and 3am
to twenty elderly alcoholics
in a testicular theme pub
on a Wednesday night
in Newcastle, New South Wales.

Punk night at the Duck's Nuts.

2000

NEWCASTLE – THE REPLAY

It's a Saturday night
in Newcastle, New South Wales,
eleven years later.
News has filtered through to me
that The Duck's Nuts
has apparently changed its name
to The Silk Bar.
But far worse news is
that the mural of the duck on a surfboard
with his testicles hanging out
has apparently been painted over.
Robina says, with a twinkle in her eye,
'Thank God it's gone!'
I think 'I've brought you
on an epic, romantic journey
to a town
on the other side of the world
to show you
a mural of a duck on a surfboard
with his testicles hanging out -
and it's been painted over.
Surely you could be more appreciative of my efforts
and sympathetic to my anguish!'

But I don't actually say that.

I'm playing at the Cambridge Hotel:
an enormous venue
in a run down area
three miles from the city centre.
According to the board outside
(the only visible publicity anywhere)
there are four bands on the bill.
Actually, there are three bands and a poet.
My friends the Go Set are headlining,
then me,
then the Sydney Girls' Choir

then the Havelocks.
At the appointed hour
for the first band
the paying audience is zero.
Even the twenty elderly alcoholics
from the Duck's Nuts
would be welcome in this cavernous void.

The Havelocks don't have locks.
(They may well have some on their guitar cases
and I'm sure they do on their front doors,
but they don't have any on their heads.)
They take to the stage to a combined audience
of myself, Robina,
and two members of the Sydney Girls' Choir.
The Havelocks appear to be in their early thirties
and sound to me
a bit like Crosby, Stills and Nash.
Their friendly singer tells me
he is originally from Staines in the UK.
I want to ask him why anybody,
even someone from Staines,
especially someone who presumably loves music,
would emigrate to Newcastle, New South Wales,
but I don't.
I think it would seem insensitive.

The Havelocks finish their set.
By this time the paying audience has risen to five.
As the next band take the stage
I can see a pattern developing.
The Havelocks don't have locks:
The Sydney Girls' Choir
aren't from Sydney,
aren't girls
and aren't a choir.
They are four blokes from Woolongong
in their early twenties
and are an excellent kick-ass rock n roll band

in a Kings of Leon meet Dr Feelgood kind of way.
The first thing the singer says
is that he is pleased to see so many people there
because they played in Newcastle last week
and nobody turned up at all.
I admire his dedication to the cause.
I join the three-strong moshpit.
I have a lovely time.

Then it's my turn.
By this time the audience has soared to about twenty
including three Attila fans,
one of whom is from Canada.
I don't think either of the other two are from Newcastle.
The void in front of me is aching.
It's monumental.
It's like being at a Crystal Palace home game.
Needless to say, I start with 'Punk Night at the Duck's Nuts'
and the sound of surreal irony echoes across the tiled savannah.
One twentieth of the audience
suddenly shouts at me.
What he shouts is 'Yabba Yabba'.
I am confused by this at first
but soon realize
that this is his way
of conveying the fact
that he is unfamiliar
with the concept of the unaccompanied spoken word
as a form of live entertainment.
I berate him, gently.
He shuts up.

In the middle of my performance
The Go Set arrive.
They've been doing another gig
at a birthday party round the corner.
I finish with a flourish
to the sound of nineteen pairs of hands
clapping in a wind tunnel

and ask my friends how their gig went.
Shithouse, I am informed.
There were 200 people there.
When the Go Set started playing
most of the guests went outside
and began dancing to techno.
The rest sat in front of them eating and chatting.
Given this,
I wonder why they were booked to do the gig
in the first place.
The people who booked them
have promised to turn up here.
I hope they will,
so I can ask them.
But they don't.

The Go Set play
I join them on fiddle
and it must be said
that the twenty-five people in the audience
have a lovely time
and are most receptive.
Afterwards, someone apologises for the turnout
and says we would have had a better crowd
if we had played somewhere else.
I agree.
They mean somewhere else in Newcastle.
I don't.

The next day
as we head out of town
we drive past what used to be the Duck's Nuts
and is now the Silk Bar.
The mural of a duck on a surfboard
with his testicles hanging out
has indeed gone.
In his stead
there is a grubby silver banner
draped on the wall

with 'The Silk Bar' written on it.
The place is now a shabby backpackers' hostel
and poking out of an upstairs window
there is something which looks worryingly
like the Antipodean equivalent
of Joseph Porter's Sleeping Bag.
Then I notice
that one of the pub signs still says
'The Duck's Nuts Hotel'.
My heart sings.
I ask Robina to take a photo.
The angle is wrong, she says.
It won't come out.
My heart sinks.
We drive away.

Back in Melbourne
I recount this tale
to my musician friend Rory.
'John' he says, earnestly,
'Newcastle is the rectum
of the Australian music scene'.
 'Rory, my old mate' I say
'I think you may be right.'

2011

THE EARLY YEARS – 1980-85
Satire was different back then. I've changed some words, left others how they were.

THEY MUST BE RUSSIANS

They slither round corners with scarves round their faces
They always turn up in improbable places
They lack the good taste of the British, our graces
They're horrid – they must be the Russians!

They're always involved in some dastardly plot
They're never content with whatever they've got
And they are the cause of the Great British Rot!
They're horrid – they must be the Russians!

They sit in the Hilton and scowl at the waiters
They drink a foul potion distilled from potatoes
And everyone knows they detest us and hate us
They're horrid – they must be the Russians!

They've Benn and the Trots who all want to enslave us
And countless Red spies who all want to deprave us
But Maggie's alright – she'll defend us and save us
From the muggers from Moscow, the Russians!

And her mate in the White House, a fine, manly figure
He knows how to handle a Jew or a ligger
When Maggie gets Trident and Ron gets the trigger
We'll give 'em deterrent, those Russians…

Oh, hang on a minute – my brain's on the blink
I think that the Kremlin's been spiking my drink
How unpatriotic – I've started to THINK!
It must all be down to the Russians…

My mate here just tells me they've got a new plan
They're holding a party in Afghanistan
And he's got an invite, as number one fan:
They can't all be horrid, the Russians!

Hey, look – over there – they're down in the park
They're holding a meeting out there in the dark
The speaker looks just like that John Cooper Clarke –
They all dress so formal, the Russians…

I'm going to meet them: I want to be friends
Find out if they follow the West's latest trends
And have long discussions, the means and the ends –
I'm getting quite fond of the Russians…

Hey, hang on – they're smiling and there's music playing!
It's punk rock – the Malchix – oh, I feel like staying!
They're handing out ice cream, and bopping, and swaying –
I THINK I'LL GO BACK WITH THE RUSSIANS!

RUSSIANS IN THE DHSS

It first was a rumour dismissed as a lie
But then came the evidence none could deny:
A double page spread in the Sunday Express –
The Russians are running the DHSS!

The scroungers and misfits have done it at last
The die of destruction is finally cast
The glue-sniffing Trotskyists' final excess:
The Russians are running the DHSS!

It must be the truth 'cos it's there in the news
A plot by the Kremlin, financed by the Jews
And set up by Scargill, has met with success –
The Russians are running the DHSS!

So go down to your Jobcentre – I bet you'll see
Albanian students get handouts for free
And drug-crazed punk rockers cavort and caress
In the interview booths in the DHSS…

They go to Majorca on taxpayers' money
Hey, you there, stop laughing – I don't think it's funny
And scroungers and tramps eat smoked salmon and cress
Now the Russians are running the DHSS!

We'll catch that rat Scargill with our red rat catcher
We'll send him to dinner with Margaret Thatcher
And we'll make him stay there until he'll confess
That he put the Reds in the DHSS!

Then we'll hang 'em and flog 'em and hang 'em again
And hang 'em and flog 'em and more of the same
We'll GAS all the dole queues and clear up the mess:
Get rid of the Reds – AND the DHSS!

RUSSIANS IN McDONALDS

Startled shoppers stand and stare
In the burger joint in Leicester Square
A cold Siberian close encounter
Muscovites behind the counter
And Georgian ladies with massive hips
Serve Breshnevburger and double chips
This is the Kremlin's latest ploy –
A difference at McDonald's you'll really enjoy!

The hammer and sickle above the door
Says Yanks not welcome any more
No more piped musak oh so dire –
Now they've a full Red Army choir
The KGB are eating in
They're kicking up a fearful din
The door guard bellows 'Shut that noise!'
The Commissar says 'Purge him, boys!'

The Stars & Stripes hang upside down
The Queen is green and wears a frown
But Lenin hangs there high and proud

Staring at the burger crowd
The American Secretary of State
An object of especial hate
Is minced and served with garlic cheese
'Cos Casper Weinburgers really please!

The Pentagon's in disarray
The news has filtered through today
And Alex Haig looks really vexed –
'The Reds'll have the Wimpys next!'
And here's more news that's really hot –
J.R. Ewing is a Trot!
Neil Diamond's played Angola –
And Marx invented Coca-Cola!

Western values fade and die
As Red successes multiply
Arthur Miller isn't dead
He's writing radio plays instead
And as the bastions crash and fall
Here comes the greatest blow of all
It took a long time to deduce
But Reagan's really... Lenny Bruce!

RUSSIANS AT THE HENLEY REGATTA

The Duchess went pallid; the Duke stood and stared
The Colonel was livid – he spluttered and glared
And the Tory Peers said, 'It's a serious matter!'
When the Russians invaded the Henley Regatta...

They charged in on DMs with football scarves high
Red soccer hooligans – 'Surrender or die!'
The Dynamo Kiev Boys, pissed out of their heads –
They kicked in the gates singing 'We are the Reds!'

They danced in the fountains and pissed in the water
(which grossly offended the Archbishop's daughter)
They nicked all the strawberries and drank the champagne –
then they took off their clothes and streaked round in the rain!

They started a ruck in the private enclosure
And Alexei got nicked for indecent exposure –
took over the Tannoy and put on the Clash
then they danced on the seats 'til they broke with a crash…

Then the Redskins turned up and they started to play
And it started a party which lasted all day
And it didn't take long for the fat cats to scatter
When the Russians invaded the Henley Regatta!

Then they jumped in the water and nicked a few yachts
And they charged off to London at thirty five knots
And for weeks all the hip clubs were filled with the chatter
Of the day that the REDS took the Henley Regatta!

RUSSIANS ON THE CENTRE COURT

Wimbledon Common is quiet today
And the Wombles are wombling the rubbish away
Old Madame Cholet is her usual self
She's quietly fingering a randy young elf
But Uncle Bulgaria's started a scare
He's just run up shouting 'Christ! Look over there…!'

His trembling finger directs all their eyes
And fear soon replaces the Wombles' surprise
For there on the common something is amiss
A massive great malchick stands having a piss
Two Soviet herberts are spraying champagne
And Vladimir is lying stoned out of his brain

Heart On My Sleeve

The RUSSIANS are here and there's no doubt of that!
Mad Leonid's wearing some old toff's top hat
That lunatic Boris is dressed up in drag
And Ivan is draped in a tatty red flag
They've just taken Henley, their greatest success
And what they'll do now is just anyone's guess!

Orinoko steps forward amidst all the fuss
And shouts 'We are the Wombles – you'll never take us!'
And 'WE ARE THE WOMBLES!' the little folk shout
But Leonid shows what the Reds are about
He squashes a Womble like he was a grub
And shouts 'Show us the way to the All England Club!'

The stands are all full at the great home of tennis
And they're quite unaware of the coming Red menace
The Men's Singles Final is well under way
When the tannoy announces suspension of play
Due to a disturbance outside at the gate
They call the police – but they've got there too late…

Vladimir and Sergei are first on the scene
Climbing over the gate shouting something obscene
As the umpires tremble all shocked and distraught
The boys from Kiev hit the great Centre Court
They sit on the turf and they swing on the net
In a scene the controller will never forget…

Sergei's got a football, and with insolent glee
Shouts 'Shengelia and Blokhin got nothing on me'
So the Soviet slobs kick the football about
Till they tread on the umpire and damage his gout
And the umpire moans, face contorted with woe
'Get rid of this lot – I prefer McEnroe!'

All the booze and the binge makes the Reds want to sleep
So they crash on the court in a great drunken heap
Till the SPG storm in and crack a few heads
And the chief of police shouts 'Right! Where are those Reds?'
But the inspector says, with a very long face
'They've gone, sir, they've vanished – gone without trace!'

And that is the truth; they're nowhere to be found
It seems like they've been swallowed up by the ground
The police check the locker rooms, toilets and bars
But then come reports of a few missing cars
And the forces of order are puzzled and vexed –
Where will those rampaging Reds show themselves next?

Will it be at the Derby, the National, the cricket?
Will they sign up with Scargill as a big flying picket?
As the Tories and faint hearts stand shocked and aghast
One thing to be sure is you ain't heard the last
So if you see a bloke with KIEV on his arm
Don't try and tackle him – sound the alarm!

RUSSIANS VERSUS THE TETLEY BITTERMEN

Down in the Charles Bronson Arms
They strangle tigers with their scarves
And pints are held in massive palms
'Cos only Southerners drink halves
They're Bradford's finest, hardest too
And in this pub you fear to tread
If you're a Cockney or a poof –
But most of all if you're a Red…

Meanwhile on the M62
The Russian hordes are Yorkshire bound
After they wrecked the Centre Court
Things got too hot to stay around
Now Wimbledon is far behind
Their nicked Ford Transit's full of beer
But Leon says 'Let's stop soon, lads –
My stomach's feeling really queer…'

'Ok' says Alex 'next turn off
We'll stop and find a quiet pub
Young Leon there can have his puke
And we'll all hit the beer and grub

But listen boys, no funny stuff –
We'll keep low profile, nice and quiet
And find a corner by the fire
I'm too hung over for a riot!'

Now we all know that History
Is oft changed by the Hand of Fate
And who can know the Destiny
That lurks unseen behind the gate?
And so it was that fateful day
When Lady Luck rang the alarms
Because the pub the eight Reds chose
Was that very same Charles Bronson Arms…

They trooped in quietly, one by one
And calmly stood there in a line
Vladimir says 'Right – it's my round –
Eight pints of Tetley's will do fine!'
But just one sip of that great brew
Makes Ivan splutter with a howl
'This stuff's the pits! It tastes like glue!
Pure wombat vomit! Really foul!'

A Bitterman snarls 'Hey, watch it, son –
Your scruffy sort aren't wanted here
Cos we eat punks with chips in gravy
Especially when they slag our beer!
And what's that tattoo on your arm?
Dynamo Kiev crew? Trotsky end?
You dirty Russky commie shit!
Get out – and take your commie friends!'

By now the Bittermen are riled
And thirty voices shout as one
'Get out of Bradford or get killed!
Go back to Russia, commie scum!'
'We don't want trouble' Georgi says
A Bitterman snarls 'Tough, Russian git!
That Gorbachov's a filthy poof
And Dynamo Kiev are SHIT!

Alexei grabs him by the throat
'That's the last straw, you fascist slobs!
You don't insult our football team –
We'll make you shut your stinking gobs!
The odds they may be ten to one
And you may think you're really tough
But lead on, Bittermen, lead on –
And damned be he who cries 'Enough!''

The memory lives in Yorkshire still
Of how the Reds evened the score
And as dawn broke in Bradford town
They kicked the Bittermen out the door
And in the Charles Bronson Arms
They do all night gay discos now.
The Bittermen won't show their face
'Cos they got splattered flat – and how!

This series was written 1979-83, the last in response to Seething Wells' infamous poem 'Tetley Bittermen'.

(And yes, I know Kiev's the capital of Ukraine. In those days 'the Russian threat' basically meant anywhere in that vague area with a hammer and sickle on it.)

A BANG & A WIMPY

A true story in verse. One of my best-known poems.

Swing door swings open in the fast food fun palace
Two pairs of eyes meet mine: I steel myself and grimace
Elbows against the counter they slump: mean-eyed, po-faced, no-nonsense
Prepubescent pugilists, terror tots, South London's finest
Knee-high nihilists planning nursery crimes
The Wimpy Bar mafia, nine years old, macho, murderous
Primary school but primed to kill, or maim, or terrorise
Size you up and slice you through with Peter Sutcliffe eyes
They're into older women – eleven or twelve's their favourite age
They chat them up as they come in, invade their space like space invaders
'Oi luv! Want some chips?' Then invite them home – for glue
And a private rendition of the new Exploited single
Or some other manic mayhem to make their extremities tingle
Soon they'll be old enough to bunk into a disco
But till then they'll stick to the hamburger hustle
A bang and a Wimpy, a Wimpy and a bang
The grim and grimy gangsters from the mustard-and-Crass gang
Video vandals, violent virgin vigilantes verging on the vindictive...
Now I've been searching for the young soul rebels
Been searching everywhere, couldn't find them anywhere
But here they are in the Wimpy bar right by Victoria Station
I stand and watch them operate in muted fascination
Till 'Ere, got ten pee, mate?' snaps me back to hard reality
And the half concealed glinting switchblade smiles with awful clarity
I give them twenty-one pence and they give me a hard smile
Now they've the price of another tube they're happy for a while
And in the Wimpy wonderland the crisis kids run free -
A bang, a Wimpy and a sniff and home in time for tea…

1981

CONTRIBUTORY NEGLIGENCE

In January 1982, at Ipswich Crown Court, an ageing High Court judge called Bertrand Richards ruled that a 17-year old female hitch hiker who was raped after thumbing a lift home from a dance hall was 'in the truest sense, asking for it' and guilty of 'contributory negligence'. The man who raped her was let off with a fine.

Hitching up the M11
Coming back from an Upstarts gig
Got picked up 'bout half eleven
By this bloke in a funny wig
Flash Mercedes, new and gleaming -
Deep pile seats and deep seat piles
I got in and sat there scheming
While the fat cat flashed me smiles…

Told me he was back from sessions
With a load of brain-dead hacks
Told me he'd made no concessions
To the bootboys and the blacks
Said he thought that it was stupid
Fuss 'bout rapists on the news
Bloke was only playing Cupid
Girls like that they don't refuse

Asked me if I thought him enemy
Asked me if I bore a grudge
Told me that he came from Henley
Said he was a High Court judge
I asked him to stop a second
'Need a slash' that's what I said
When he did the anger beckoned
And I smacked him in the head

Heart On My Sleeve

Took the keys and took his money
Crashed the car into a ditch
Though he moaned 'They'll get you, sonny!'
Got away without a hitch
I don't think they'll ever find me
'Cos I'm many miles away
But if one day they're right behind me
I know what I'm gonna say –

HE ASKED FOR IT! He's rich and snobbish
Right wing, racist, sexist too!
Brain dead, stupid, sick and slobbish –
Should be locked in London Zoo!
He wanted me to beat him up!
It was an open invitation!
Late at night he picked me up –
An act of open provocation!

High Court judges are a blight –
They should stay home in nice warm beds
And if they must drive late at night
Should never pick up Harlow Reds!
A five pence fine is right and proper
And to sum up my defence
It was his fault he came a cropper –
CONTRIBUTORY NEGLIGENCE!

AWAYDAY

In October 1981, as part of their election manifesto, Ken Livingstone's Greater London Council reduced London tube and bus fares by 31% to encourage greater use of public transport and reduce traffic problems: it was a hugely popular and successful measure, and was challenged in an act of sheer political spite by Tory-controlled Bromley Council. Five Law Lords led by Lord Denning ruled that the entire scheme was illegal, and in March 1982, the GLC were forced to double the fares. Once more, there was uproar at a 'judicial' decision made by elderly upper-class males who appeared completely out of touch with ordinary people and their lives. A campaign was launched, and many people refused to pay the increased fares. Badges and stickers were everywhere: 'I voted for cheap fares. Who voted for Lord Denning?' My contribution was a cautionary tale about the perils of a day out in London with the Law Lords...

Woke up got up read the post attacked the postman took the rat for a walk came back fed the amoeba made some coffee wrote a passionate love letter to shirley williams enclosing a small dead animal then thought i'm bored think I'll go to london 'cos london's more interesting than harlow and i might be able to pick up some buck's fizz bootlegs or the latest jean-paul sartre dub lp got the bus ten minutes late got the train twenty minutes late train was delayed for two hours due to dead liberals on the line got to london liverpool street went down the tube stepping on unsuspecting commuters all the way up to the ticket booth single to covent garden please sure mate that'll be five pound fifty what do you mean five pound fifty it was only twenty pence yesterday i'm not paying five pound fifty to go to covent garden from liverpool street sorry mate i know it was only twenty pence yesterday but a ninety seven year old deaf geriatric ostrich-minded extremely rich archaic obsolete semi-senile reactionary friedman-worshipping member of an outdated unnecessary and entirely superfluous elitist and oligarchic institution who never uses the tube anyway 'cos he's got a fucking chauffeur-driven limousine woke up with a headache in the middle of last night and decided to increase london transport fares by two thousand percent and got four of his senile friends to agree with him – posthumously – and so we've had to put the fares up that's called freedom democracy the rule of law and defending the british way of life that'll be five pound fifty please…

BOLLOCKS TO THAT i said and after a short pregnant pause all the people in the queue plucked up courage and said BOLLOCKS TO THAT and all the pinstripe-and-soda brigade coming down the stairs said BOLLOCKS TO THAT and all the other people at liverpool street underground and at the bus stops said BOLLOCKS TO THAT apart from the nice polite human league and haircut one hundred fans who thought it was rude to say BOLLOCKS but when it was revealed to them that in the famous sex pistols LP cover trial of 1977 a high court judge had ruled that BOLLOCKS was not an obscene word then they too said BOLLOCKS TO THAT and soon the entire length and breadth of the london transport network was full of people saying BOLLOCKS TO THAT and refusing to pay the increased fares and when finally a large crowd of completely sober and totally moderate forty nine year old lloyds underwriters called Brian started going up to yer average law lord in the street saying BOLLOCKS TO THAT and hitting him over the head with a large mallet then the powers that be decided to abandon the fares increase in the interest of public safety then everything went back to normal but it made me wonder so i'm forming a mass revolutionary party and our slogan manifesto and programme is going to be BOLLOCKS TO THAT!

NIGEL WANTS TO GO TO C&A'S

A surreal poem based on a snippet of conversation between some passers-by I'd overheard in an Oxford shopping centre. Yes, I know it should be 'C&A' not 'C&A's'. But that's what was said – and this is what I thought….

Nigel wants to go to C&A's
but it's been taken over by the Viet Cong
and Nigel doesn't like the Viet Cong

Nigel wants to go to C&A's
but a chapter of Hell's Angels are playing Scrabble
with the Viet Cong
and Nigel doesn't like Hell's Angels

Nigel wants to go to C&A's
but the toilets are full of Crass fans
and Nigel doesn't like Crass fans

Nigel wants to go to C&A's
but the Women's Institute have organised an orgy
in the bedding department
and Nigel doesn't like orgies

Nigel wants to go to C&A's
but the lifts are full of Albanian footballers
and Nigel doesn't like Albanian footballers

Nigel wants to go to C&A's
but the menswear department is full of existentialists
and Nigel doesn't like existentialists
not even part-time ones

Nigel wants to go to C&A's
But I don't understand why
'cos they don't sell nerve gas in C&A's
- not even to SDP members in cashmere sweaters…

1982

NIGEL WANTS TO GO AND SEE SIMPLE MINDS

Nigel wants to go and see Simple Minds
They're playing at the Camden Palace
and Nigel likes the Camden Palace

Nigel wants to go and see Simple Minds
They're supporting the Smiths
and Nigel likes the Smiths
(Though not as much as Simple Minds)

Nigel wants to go and see Simple Minds
The singer's got a funny voice
and Nigel likes funny voices

Nigel wants to go and see Simple Minds
The singer's got a funny haircut
and Nigel likes funny haircuts

Nigel wants to go and see Simple Minds
They play nice, bland, unchallenging pop music
and Nigel likes nice, bland, unchallenging pop music
That's why he likes Simple Minds

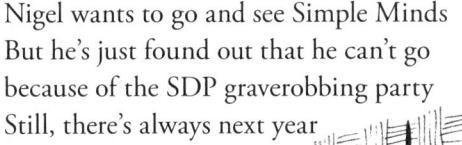

Nigel wants to go and see Simple Minds
But he's just found out that he can't go
because of the SDP graverobbing party
Still, there's always next year

1982

I DON'T TALK TO POP STARS

I don't talk to pop stars
and they don't talk to me
it's a mutual arrangement –
the way we like to be
I don't talk to pop stars
they make me feel depressed
and I won't sit in dressing rooms
and watch them get undressed
I don't talk to pop stars
they really piss me off
I hope they die in poverty
like poor Vincent van Gogh
I don't talk to pop stars
and I hope that you don't too
'Cos if you've talked to Billy Bragg
then I won't talk to you
I don't talk to pop stars
won't share their cans of beer
I never nick their underpants
I'd better make that clear
I don't talk to pop stars
I think they should be shot
or gassed, or hung, or sterilized
or the whole bloody lot
I don't talk to pop stars
they really make me sick
especially that Seething Wells
he really is a prick
I don't talk to pop stars
They really make me vomit
I'd rather clean out lavatories
Or study Halley's comet

Heart On My Sleeve

I don't talk to pop stars
I wish they'd go away
and I walk out of pop concerts
when pop stars start to play
I don't talk to pop stars
but listen to my plea
one day when I'm a pop star
will you still talk to me?

1982

THE NIGHT I SLEPT WITH SEETHING WELLS
The last line is very poignant.

A far off town and a late night bash
And a double bed was our place to crash
So listen here – 'cos this story tells
Of the night I slept with Seething Wells!

I didn't mind – or so I said
But I wish I'd had the floor instead
Cos you'd never imagine the thousand hells
Of a night in bed with Seething Wells...

When he got undressed I had to retreat
From his shaven head and his mouldy feet
The feet that launched a thousand smells
In that fragrant night with Seething Wells

So I kept right close to the edge of the bed
And I pulled the blankets over my head
But eerie snores and stifled yells
Soon woke me, thanks to Seething Wells

And, turning, I came face to face
With a massive boil in a private place
And a couple of hairy bagatelles
Made me run like hell from Seething Wells!

And I vowed right then that if need be
I'd spend the night in a cemetery
Or sleep with dogs, or DEAD GAZELLES -
But never again with Seething Wells!

1981

THE PERILS OF STEALING HALF A BOTTLE OF WINE

Michael Fagan, a friendly but eccentric soul, pays a personal visit to the Queen in her own bedroom at Buckingham Palace and steals half a bottle of wine. All hell breaks loose. And yes, forty years ago, I used to drink Fosters sometimes. I grew out of it.

Three o'clock in the afternoon feeling really pissed off the jean-paul sartre dub lp featuring jah schopenhauer is awful and the bucks fizz bootlegs aren't bucks fizz at all they're crass live at the tory party conference and to crown it all there isn't even any albanian football on the telly right i think i'll go and get drunk i've never done that before pubs aren't open so it's down to the off licence past c&a's hello nigel no nigel put that nail bomb away i'm not the prat who writes nasty things about you into the off licence ten crates of fosters and half a bottle of white wine for my pet halibut maxwell on the way to the checkout desk realise i haven't got enough money so i slip the wine under my jacket and smile sweetly at the till operator all goes well until i trip over the serious poetry reading being held by the door and crash forward revealing the offending bottle you thieving scum shouts the shop manager i'll have your scrotal sac for this as he holds me in a vice like grip and dials the police with his free hand ten meat wagons three armoured cars a detatchment of the sas and five harrier jump jets storm the building and as i'm seized and taken into custody i'm astonished at the commotion until i realise that i'm going to be charged with stealing half a bottle of wine and the going rate for that is three years of intensive electric shock treatment and ice baths in solitary confinement followed by twenty years in the mental hospital of your choice with the option of being experimented on in a vivisection clinic and playing endless games of chess with sterilised monkeys so I think to myself as i'm led away that next time i won't steal half a bottle of wine i'll try something less dangerous like tax embezzlement property speculation or fraud 'cos no one worries about things like that do they..

1982

GENTLEMEN OF THE WRIST
Another rant dating from my eleven months in the Stock Exchange...

In a shitty city wine bar whining in their wine about rates and dates and druggers and muggers and red ken and his men and dirty diners and militant miners they slob out the evening in sweaty pinheaded pinstriped pissed up pathetic postures paranoid penpushers on parole gin and tonic really chronic quite moronic want to be bionic but whoever heard of a bionic bank clerk wouldn't that be a lark the nightly convention of the highly conventional order of the gentlemen of the wrist brackets pissed spews the news and blows a fuse they whinge and binge and singe their minge eric should have been home two hours ago his wife will kill him but it's his round so he's staying around the eighth pint's been downed and the first one to be sick is a prick so give it some stick mick 'cos eric's a real man and he can hold his lukewarm watneys better than you can heard the one about the queer irish jew locked in the loo ha ha great mate give us another before we go home to one mother or another look over there that bird is the word could really poke that no don't be an absurd nerd don't be a twat that's too fat time to go see you tomorrow have a good pube on the tube but watch out for the liggers and the triggers and the nightly convention of the highly conventional order of the gentlemen of the wrist brackets pissed is dismissed home to the wife who says hello little jife where have you been you smell obscene it's plainly seen you're no james dean four hours late food's on the plate i didn't wait hero zero eight hours work five hours drinking five seconds thinking time for sleep for suburban sheep off to bed empty head might as well be dead!

1982

Boyds Sperm Bank
Splashpoint
NOTICE
WITHDRAWAL ONLY.
NO DEPOSIT!

Attila The Stockbroker

MY WARDROBE
My reaction to the verse of some of the poets I met in my early years as Attila...

My wardrobe is like a garden
but there's jackets instead of the snails
and instead of the trees there's jeans with no knees
and instead of the birdshit there's rails

My wardrobe is like a garden
but there's hangers instead of the grass
and instead of the fence there's a stray twenty pence
in a suit with a hole in the arse

My wardrobe is like a garden
But there's Y fronts instead of the dirt
And instead of the stems there's a pair of DMs
And instead of the leaves there's a shirt

My wardrobe is like a garden
But instead of the flowers there's socks
And instead of the heather there's vests made of leather
And a whip that I keep in a box

My wardrobe is like a garden.
Oh, I don't know how I've got the gall.
My wardrobe is just like a wardrobe.
It's not like a garden at all!

1982

DEATH in BROMLEY

DEATH IN BROMLEY

Deep in the dingy dirty decomposing dogshit-dripping dungeon of a graffiti-graced southern region train compartment stuffed full of bad-breath-breathing halibut-eyed computer commuters with boring suits and boring habits the state of play is giving cause for concern the middle-aged-middle-class-middle-management-middle-everything-puke-suited-slack-jawed-suet-pudding-faced-thatcher-worshipping willie whitelaw clone by the window is slumped rigidly over his daily telegraph in a posture indicating his sudden demise this alarms the prim po-faced-clean-tablecloth-every-night-daily-mail-female secretary by his side who asks him politely if he recently died receiving no reply she turns to the lard-arsed-times-reading-tory-voting pinstriped wimp sitting opposite and demands an opinion in company with the three paul eddington clones also occupying the compartment he lowers his eyes and stares fixedly at his newspaper in the time honoured fashion of the don't-pinch-my-seat-don't-invade-my-world-i'm-alright-jack-leave-me-alone English suburban commuter husbands club she turns to me and confidently i tell her that most commuters are dead it's their natural state and anyway dead executives can't possibly be any less interesting than live ones though i can see that they might smell a bit more and that's why they always get aftershave for Christmas and anyway I'm never going to bromley again unless i become an undertaker or join the SDP which is roughly the same thing...

1982

VIDEO NAZIS

A response to the promotion of ghastly misogynistic 'horror films' in the mid 1980s New Musical Express.

In Rome the gladiators fought
while people slobbered in the stands
the bloodlust rose, the voyeurs wanked
with transfixed gaze and frenzied hands
then naked humans thrown to beasts
were torn apart amidst the cheers
their last entreaties drowned in blood
and wine-soaked sick sadistic jeers

And so it swells, the evil lust
centuries old and still unslaked
the cesspit of the human mind
the vampire free, unchained, unstaked
and now sick men – it's always men –
are harnessing the stinking vulture
lurking in the human soul
and flaunting it as video culture

Film makers, impotent and scared
with shrivelled pricks and sick desires
hate women so they stab their breasts
or wrench their nipples off with pliers
and hipsters in the music press
say 'What's the fuss? It's special effects!'
It's real enough in those bastards' minds –
I want to break their fucking necks!

And what of those who watch the films
of Nazis raping Jewish mothers:
do they sit there, and wank, and spout
wish they were there beside the others –
then play with children of their own
as SS butchers used to do?
Look in the mirror, nasty fan –
See Adolf Eichmann stare at you!

1985

ANDY IS A CORPORATIST

Recorded over a dub version of the Newtown Neurotics' 'Mindless Violence' and released on an 'Oi' album to put clueless idiots straight. It worked, though I got in a few scrapes at gigs as a result.

Andy is a corporatist
He is corpulent, often pissed
And he is friends with Flemish nazis
Goes to Hitler's birthday parties
(Seven times a year....)
I met him at the 100 Club
He was there on business
But he couldn't start a riot
So he stayed kinda quiet
And the Business didn't play
So Andy went away
I met him in Birmingham
The day the shit really hit the fan
The fan was me and the shit was Andy –
Upstarts concert, really handy
Broken nose is really dandy
Andy thinks it's such a laugh
To sing Horst Wessel in the bath
Smash up other people's fun
Make page 20 of the Sun
But I knew his time would come...
Andy's mate came up today
Told me he'd been put away
'Stupid nutter, anyway!'
That's all he said, then turned away.

A year of life went down the drain
Then they let Andy out again
The guys inside had changed his mind -
He'd left his fascist past behind
One day I met him in the pub
He'd finished with the killing club
He said he had to watch his face
'Cos you don't leave the master race..

Attila The Stockbroker

Now Andy and his local crew
Stand firm against the chosen few
He's playing in a rebel band
To spread the word across the land
And sometimes, in a pissed–up haze,
He talks about the bad old days
And here's his message, loud and clear:
'WE'LL NEVER LET IT HAPPEN HERE!
You Nazi boneheads ought to know
That you would be the first to go
'Cos what they want is serried ranks
Unsmiling clones in Chieftain tanks
No room for music, punk or skin –
They'll bring the goosestep marchers in
And take our football and our bands
Smash our guitars and break our hands
So no more crap about colour of skin
'Cos unity's the way to win!'
And what our Andy says is true:
Stand firm – don't let them hoodwink you!

1982

THE ORACLE
(a slightly rude nonsensical sound poem, included on my first EP for Cherry Red Records)

A bloke who works for Pinnacle a firm that's really cynical asked me to write an article and make it really radical i know it sounds improbable and practically impossible but writing up the article i sat upon my testicle and found a little particle of testicle on the article i got a small receptacle and took it to the hospital where they looked very sceptical they said that's not a testicle it looks like a comestible you blokes are so predictable the nurse said looking cynical while waiting in the vestibule of the septic sceptic hospital a spider seized my testicle and munched it in its mandible the pain sent me hysterical it really was incredible so i clutched my aching testicle and yelled for something medical the nurse was still quite cynical as she bandaged up my testicle no need to be hysterical she said applying chemical the bandage was impractical and it exposed my oracle so the looks i got were quizzical as i left the local hospital a pig in a convertible with a mate who looked identical and really quite irascible said cover up your oracle i said it was impractical because i'd hurt my testicle and if he still was sceptical he ought to ask the hospital the particle of testicle still rested on the article which i had done for Pinnacle the firm that's really cynical the article was radical and really quite street credible and though it sounds incredible the particle was edible the one conclusion logical was that the little particle was not part of my testicle but was a small comestible as they said in the hospital by now you must be cynical this rant's become predictable and so I'll end this canticle this tale of tortured testicle mistaken for comestible I'll finish with an oracle it really is impossible to try and write an article while sitting on your testicle it makes you go HYSTERICAL!

1982

A VERY SILLY EASTERN EUROPEAN PROPAGANDA STATION

I discovered Radio Tirana's English broadcasts in the early 70s because they interfered with Radio One on 247 medium wave. Soon I was hooked: my early years as Attila were infested with Albanian references. This is what the broacasts sounded like, very slightly satirised – but only slightly…

Long live the People's Socialist Republic of Albania under the correct leadership of the Party of Labour of Albania with Comrade Enver Hoxha at the head!

Long live the steel-like unity of the Albanian workers, peasants and people's intellectuals around their beloved Party as they carry forward the bright red banner of socialism and win ever more brilliant victories in the construction of the socialist homeland!

Glory to Marxism-Leninism, an ever-correct and scientific doctrine and an iron-forged weapon in the hands of the progressive peoples!

Death to American imperialism, Soviet social-imperialism, Chinese revisionism, colonialism, neo-colonialism and the traitorous activities of the Yugoslav revisionist plotters, their lackeys, running dogs and HALIBUTS!

Long live Comrade Enver Hoxha, beloved son of the Albanian soil, and his pet flounder, TRISTAN!

Victory to people's war and the liberation movements of the world under the correct leadership of RODDY THE RAGWORM!

Long live people's electrification, socialist collectivisation and LARRY THE LUGWORM!

The wombats have nothing to lose but their bondage trousers! Wombats of all countries, UNITE!

And to end our very silly broadcast, here is a poem.
Stalin had a little lamb
It gave him naughty urges
So he tied it to a five bar gate
And shot it in the purges…

1983

Heart On My Sleeve

THE STATE OF THINGS

TROT ZOMBIE TAKEOVER APOCALYPSE!
A rewrite of 'Russians in the DHSS' 35 years later...

It first was a rumour dismissed as a lie
But then came the evidence none could deny
Tom Watson revealed it on the BBC -
Dead Russians are running the Labour Party!

The plotters and entrists have done it at last
The die of destruction is finally cast…
We don't think for ourselves, we're controlled by Trotsky -
Dead Russians are running the Labour Party!

He seems quite unfazed by the fact that he's dead
With an ice pick stuck jauntily into his head
He says 'Leon the Zombie supports Jeremy….'
Dead Russians are running the Labour Party!

It must be the truth 'cos it's there in the news:
Despite being Jewish, he tells us 'Hate Jews -
And brick people's windows.' Oh no! Deary me!
Dead Russians are running the Labour Party!

With his crap goatee beard and his poncy pince-nez
He tells thousands of young Corbyn fans 'You obey
My Transitional Programme, or you'll get no tea…'
Dead Russians are running the Labour Party!

But Jeremy's got a coalition that's broad.
Does the media not know we've got Stalin on board?
And there's old Ra Ra Rasputin too, so that's three
Dead Russians a-running the Labour Party!

An end to this madness! Please, spin doctor now!
Oh give me dark suit, give me serious brow!
Give me same old same old, and a nice cup of tea….
Dead Russians are running the Labour Party!

2016

Heart On My Sleeve

REPOSSESSED BY THE DEVIL

In the days of the old never-never
when your house rose in price with each day
in a right to buy giveaway con-trick
to make millions vote Margaret's way
you mortgaged your income to Satan
Doctor Faustus of Shoreham-by-Sea
saw the homeless in the bed and breakfasts
and thought how the hell can that be…
Yes, you borrowed the earth in the eighties
when the plastic explosion held sway
Your repayments are late so this is your fate –
Repossessed by the devil today

You used to be prudent and thrifty
till Satan's slaves took you in hand
'You are what you buy!' was the corporate cry
in a don't pay till next year land
No matter you're stretched to the limit –
to our credit we'll offer you more
but now all the chickens have come home to roost –
there are men in grey minds at the door
You were top of the tree in the eighties
when the plastic explosion held sway
You bought crap on a whim now you're out on a limb
repossessed by the devil today

In the London hotels where the suits go to lunch
if you beg your way into the feast
You'll see Major, the devil's trainspotter
and the chancellor, neighbour of the beast
making jokes with their friends in the City
whose promises put you in hock
and talking of regeneration
while the bailiffs are changing the lock
But again you believed what they told you
on your hand-picked excursion to hell
'It's better the devil you know, mate'
Now you've got to know him far too well…

1991

APRIL FOOL IN SEPTEMBER

All in vain.
A total waste of everything.
You'll never know - that's the point.
You'll never, ever know.
Because you killed yourselves
and all those people
and that was that.
Quite literally, for you and for them,
end of story.
All in vain.
Your mothers' pain in childbirth,
the love of your families,
your growth, your education,
a complete waste of time.
The transition, if you want to call it that
from soft-handed sons of bourgeois parents
to your new way:
born of rage
rage at the filthy injustices perpetrated on your people
by the money thugs of the West
rage which thirty years before would have led you to
the bright red banner with the hammer and sickle of hope
to the Soviet Union and its training camps
to Marx, to Lenin, to the global liberation movements
but which now led you to…
nothing.
Conviction, conversion,
prostration before your 'god',
decision, training -
then those final few days.
Your last savourings of whatever it was in life you loved the most.
The touch of a woman, perhaps?
Although somehow I doubt that:
You hated women, didn't you -
One of you went as far as to leave instructions
that no woman should ever visit his grave..
Your last drink. Your last meal.

The unbearable tension as you went through the checks.
Then the elation of success, control, power!
All for nothing.

Brutality on board,
slashing, beating:
the beseeching, cringing victims
phoning their loved ones
for the very last time
and then the moment
when you approached
those sterile momuments to Mammon
full of living human beings
many of them poorer and more screwed down by the money power
than you had ever been
bared your chests, welcomed your 'god'-
and then you found out.
Or rather, you didn't.
You just died.
Your tissue, your existence immolated in one split second
And then - oblivion.
The indescribable nightness of not being.
No Paradise, no life after death,
No martyrs, no holy war, nothing.
Just oblivion...
and the sobs of the bereaved.

Now I go back.
Back to Gorbachev, cringing before capital.
Back to the people dancing on the Berlin Wall,
then crashing off, to find no safety net below,
just the merciless sneers of the West.
Back to the day the poor, the oppressed, the brutalised of the world were told
'The Red Flag has been lowered!
MacSociety has won!
Welcome to the New World Order!'
Justice hungry people left without Marx's standard
and a Western backed spawn of clerics
there to fill the void

and twist the minds of a generation of dupes
into the walking bombs of today
- walking into nothing.
Hey, America!
In the 80s you armed them in Afghanistan.
In the 90s you armed them in Bosnia.
Now they fly to your citadel
and bite the hand that feeds.
April Fool, America!
April Fool, Islamic 'martyr!'
April Fool in September.
April Fool.

Written after the events of 11 September 2001

NEVER FORGET

Written after I was asked to compere the 'Orgreave Mass Picnic' commemorating the 30th anniversary of the Battle of Orgreave on 18 June 1984. We were buzzed by a police helicopter that day. Dedicated to the Orgreave Truth and Justice Campaign.

I remember my stepfather moaning
In the first strike in '72
'Miners holding the country to ransom...'
I was fourteen. I thought about you.
You worked underground, often in danger.
Hewed the coal we depended upon.
He earned more checking tax forms in Brighton.
I knew then just whose side I was on.

I remember Kent pickets at Shoreham
When our port bosses shipped in scab coal.
By the time they were back twelve years later
A new anger burned deep in my soul.
You'd won once, but this time would be harder
For your foe was no bumbling Heath.
It was Thatcher, revenge her agenda.
A class warrior, armed to the teeth.

You were miners on strike for your future:
For your pits, your communities, ways.
We were punks, poets, anarchists, lesbians.
Theatre groups, Rastafarians, gays.
Different worlds in a rainbow alliance
Fired up and determined to win.
And Thatcher lumped us all together:
Punk or miner. The enemy within.

As a poet, I crisscrossed the country
From Durham to Yorkshire to Kent.
Doing benefits, arguing, learning.
Raising funds that were so quickly spent.
Playing a tiny role in that great battle
That you fought so hard and to the last.
A battle so proudly remembered
Now that thirty long years have passed.

Heart On My Sleeve

I remember those pictures from Orgreave.
Police faces contorted with hate.
The communities brutalized, shattered
By the raw, naked power of the state.
If it took guns and tanks to defeat you
She'd have used guns and tanks on you too.
The veneer of democracy shattered.
The hired thugs of the privileged few.

After Orgreave came Wapping, then Hillsborough.
With the press and police on her side
Thatcher smiled as the printers were beaten
And those ninety six football fans died.
She had a quite open agenda
Summed up well when she famously said
That there's no such thing as society.
Don't blame us for being pleased that she's dead.

Now the bankers destroy the economy
And the poor and the sick get the blame
And our once mighty, proud labour movement
Is shackled, and timid, and tame
But this poet will always remember
All the brave men and women I met
We will carry on fighting for justice –

And we'll never, no never, forget.

2014

THERESA THE APPEASER

Theresa the Appeaser
Met the lady garden squeezer.
Her brain was in the freezer -
She treated him like Caesar!
He's a really dodgy geezer
So tell Queen Liz, if he sees her,
'Grab his knob with a tweezer
And revoke his sodding visa!'

A TALE OF THREE BUSHES

Thatcher met Bush senior.
Blair met Bush no-hoper.
But May has drawn the short straw.
She just met Bush groper.

2016

A MAN OF HIS WORD

It is unusual for a contemporary politician to keep, or even attempt to keep, promises made during election campaigns. Unfortunately, Trump appears to be bucking the trend.

As the last Trump
exploded from the febrile rectum
of the loathsome demagogue
enveloping all before him
in a stinking fog of bigotry and hatred
he turned to the cameras
and spoke.
'My fellow Americans:
During my election campaign
I made you some promises.
Here are three of them.
I promised to build a wall.
To ban Muslims.
To end Obamacare.
I want to keep those promises.
I aim to follow through…
All over America.'

2016

MY DOCTOR MARTENS

I was about sixteen
when I bought my first pair.
Cherry red, like that Groundhogs song
and the lovely record label named after it
which published my early albums
and, more than thirty years later,
my autobiography.
Since then we've had
the same relationship
as Tories have with the poor and disadvantaged -
I've looked down on them constantly.
This poet has measured out his life
not with coffee spoons
but lace hole numbers
and his cherry blossom
has always come
in a tin.

The number of holes diminished
as the years advanced.
In the ska wars
of the seventies and eighties
when Babylon burned
the skrewdriver twisted
and we stared at the rude boys
in a ghost town called malice
there were twelve -
with turn-ups to show them off.
They were my Trident.
A sensible deterrent
which cost twenty quid, not billions
and when it failed
as it occasionally did
caused minor local damage
to some bigoted bonehead bully
rather than blowing up the whole planet.

Of course, there was the odd bit of incoming fire
when the jackboot was on the other foot
and the smell of brown leather
blended in with the weather -
but I'm here to tell the tale.

Time passed.
We thought: plenty more battles
but that one's over.
We've rocked and rucked against racism
and won.
By the middle nineties
there were ten holes
then eight or six
and now, in the summer at least,
I mostly wear the shoes.
A couple of years ago
I found a pair of twelves
in a long-unexplored cupboard.
Songs and faces came into my head
I smiled
and my wife took them to the charity shop
where she works.

On Friday, 9th November 2016
the day Trump was 'elected' president
with a minority of the popular vote
five months after the chaos of Brexit
the racists crowed
and the internet threats began again.
'Enjoy it while it lasts -
We will crush you, traitor'.
Although I am 62 years old
I wished those twelve hole DMs
were still in the cupboard.
But I still have the eight
and the six.

I don't want to fight anyone -
I never have -
but we will not bow to this hatred.
We didn't win after all.
Get your boots on, folks.
It's starting again.
It's starting again.

2016 - slightly updated

SUPERMODEL

Prepubescent imagery.
Empty, stupid eyes.
Waif thin.
Tyrannical.
No fat.
No body hair.
No character, no love, no personality -
no brain.
So thin, and yet…
so thick.
By your anodyne complicity
in this gruesome stereotype
you connive
in the corporate enslavement of your sisters
- anorexia, bulimia, self-loathing, fear.
They aspire to be like you
- an unnatural creation of capital -
and wreck their bodies in the process,
destroy their fertility,
tear apart their lives.
But hang on a minute?
Not my place to talk about that?
I'm a man, what do I know?
You're just trying to earn a living?
What I'm saying has been said before?
OK.
But when the football blokes look
and make some expected remark
I'm supposed to join in.
I'm supposed to fancy you -
or pretend to.
Well, I don't.
And I won't.
More than that.
You revolt me.
You give me an inversion.
It's quite simple really.

I just don't desire a stupid adman's toy
styled to look like a prepubescent girl
- a real 'babe' -
there in the tabloid
next to the lurid description
of Gary Glitter's downfall.
I love a real woman.

I won't buy the product you advertise.
I won't watch your latest film.
I'm not interested in your poxy TV series
I'll never set foot in that fucking car
and I hate you.
I know I should just ignore you, or feel sorry for you
but I hate you
and your fashionist masters
bringers of misery
destroyers of individuality
harbingers of despair.
Women and men:
Riot against diet!
Sod the microchip revolution -
let's have a fish 'n' chip one!
Cream bun chocolate cream bun chocolate
lard lard sag aloo beer beer beer!
Riot against diet!
Smash fashionism!
Say goodbye to Hello!
Make Cosmopolitan....cosmopolitan!
Let's have a real woman's realm!
Take over the curry house
Fill your freezer full of ice cream
Live
Love
Get real!

2014

A HELLISH ENCOUNTER
Written shortly after the death of Margaret Thatcher

The furnaces were roaring
With a foul and sulphurous smell
The damned were being tortured –
Just another day in Hell.
The air was full of ghastly screams
And soul-destroying moans
When above the dreadful clamour
Rose some shrill suburban tones…

'So messy! And so smelly!
And so awfully, awfully hot!
And all you do is torture –
That puts nothing in the pot!
I'll close down all your furnaces
Your unproductive ways
And build a brand new call centre –
A Purgatory that pays!'

The Devil dropped his pitchfork
And put on his coat and hat.
'I don't mind facing Jesus
But I can't compete with that!'
But the damned and all the goblins
Pleaded 'Lucifer, don't go!'
Stay and help us in our fight -
Better the Devil that we know!'

So they voted him shop steward
And he led a demonstration
While Thatcher glared and tutted
In mad, impotent frustration.
Then they made some massive banners
In huge letters: 'COAL NOT DOLE'!
'NOT ONE SINGLE FURNACE CLOSURE!'
'GO TO HEAVEN, TORY TROLL!'

Now Tomas de Torquemada
Held a centuries-old position
As editor of Hell's newspaper –
The Daily Inquisition.
So Thatcher went to him and said
'I need some press support.
You always do my bidding.
Here's some text for your report!'

But Tomas said 'Can't help you -
'Cos, Satan, he's my mate!
You know I've served him faithfully
Since 1498…'
So she yelled upstairs to Murdoch:
'Rupert, time for you to die!
I need you down here urgently!'
But there was no reply.

Then the Devil came in glory
Brian Clough at his right hand
And in tones to shatter marble
Thundered: 'Margaret, you are banned!
Hell's a worker-run collective
Self-sufficient, closely-knit.
We don't need your poxy meddling.
I condemn you to the pit!

But, first, I'll reunite you
With the one you love the most.
He was hiding in the coal hole.
He was dressed up as a ghost.
Said he DIDN'T WANT to see you!
Said to PLEASE keep him away!
But you're here now, aren't you, Denis?
Bid your lady wife good day…'

Heart On My Sleeve

They were taken to the lift shaft
And soon they were gone from sight
And heading for an awful place
Of pain and endless night
And you're not going to believe this
'Twas such awful, rotten luck -
 But half way down the endless pit
The Thatchers' lift got stuck...

So fight for social justice
And build a better world
And bury her foul legacy
With red banners unfurled
And heed the final message
Of this cautionary verse
Or you could end up like Denis.
I can think of nothing worse.

2013

CARRIAGE H
For Richard Castle, survivor of the Paddington train disaster

Not the normal victims -
not this time.
Not the forgotten people:
the ones who put you there,
ground down now as before,
eighteen years of misery,
countless more of betrayal.
Theirs is a routine, everyday suffering.
You're used to that:
hospital waiting list, neighbourhood terror,
fuel poverty, the usual things.
You know how to deal with them.
They are sent to a spin doctor
and forgotten, along with their votes:
after all, you say,
they've nowhere else to go...
But it wasn't them.
Not this time.
An unusually comprehensive capitulation
to the moneylenders in the temple
even by your nice, Middle England, church-on-Sunday-and-shit-on-thy-neighbour
'modernising' ecumenical standards, Mr. Blair.
This time, your friends connived
in the murder of some of their own -
for, yes, it was a first class inferno
in Carriage H.
And though safety before profit
and renationalisation without compensation
would bring a belly cheer of relief and hope
from everyone who entrusts their living bodies
to these everyday cylinders on wheels
and such a measure
would be one of the most popular governmental decisions
in British political history
you remain loyal.
Loyal as the puppet to the hand.

Heart On My Sleeve

Loyal to the faceless, murderous thugs of capital
who lurk behind every New Labour smile.
The IMF. The City. The banks.
You don't care about us.
You dance on the graves of the Paddington dead
with talk of tube privatisation
and air traffic control privatisation
- the vapid sheep say nothing
and those who speak the truth
are called extremists.
And even after Hatfield and Potters Bar
when the country is crying out for justice
when police want to prosecute
the filthy profiteering scum
who murder our people
you do nothing.
My kind of Labour government
would renationalise the railways without compensation
imprison the entire board of Railtrack
and try them,
not for corporate manslaughter,
but for crimes agains the people,
repoen the Northwich salt mines
and send them to slave there for life
with loop tapes of Phil Collins' greatest hits
and slow motion videos of Crystal Palace reserve games
as their only respite.
You are not my kind of Labour government.
I want something else.
And I want it now.

1999

ATTILA THE STOCKBROKER CLEANS UP THE CITY

I was a clerk there: I've seen the greed
How wealth and power eat hope and need
Now they're eating each other but they're still screaming
'No interference' – I start dreaming…
'Self regulation?' OK, I say
'I'm a stockbroker – let's do it my way'
And that's the beginning of this little ditty:
Attila the Stockbroker cleans up the City!

Each gets a red nose so everybody knows
Just who they are and where all our money goes
No more speculate, no more accumulate -
This is a lifestyle we're going to eradicate
Dealers on the floor meet squads of the poor saying
'Here's the twist, Oliver – we want more
Work for us or we take the whole kitty'
Attila the Stockbroker cleans up the City!

'Hello Mr. Hedge Fund, have a cup of tea.
Financial Services Authority? Me.
You're a parasite on the population
Convicted of criminal speculation
Time to atone for a life so greedy -
Twenty years working for the poor and needy.
Want to appeal? Try the Central Committee…'
Attila the Stockbroker cleans up the City!

Morning Mr Banker, you're in for a shock.
We're taking much more than just Northern Rock!
All the banks nationalised – Stock Exchange too.
Utilities, railways, grabbed from the few.
Mr Billionaire? You just lost your money.
(Hey there, Chelsea fan, isn't that funny!)
The future's brown. The future's shitty.
So Attila the Stockbroker cleans up the City!

Heart On My Sleeve

Capitalism is a John Cleese parrot.
Let's give it stick and not a single carrot!
Bollocks to the dealer, the broker, the lender -
Social justice back on the agenda
Radical solutions going on here
Smoked Mammon sarnies and really good beer
For the poor no fear, for the rich no pity
When Attila the Stockbroker cleans up the City!

2011

A DIET OF MAINSTREAM MEDIA

'Burnt toast gives you cancer.
White bread does the same.
So do chips and bacon –
Corbyn is to blame.'

Turkeys vote for Christmas
When told to by the press.
That's why this fucking country
Is in such a fucking mess.

2019

AT NO PARLIAMENTARY EXPENSE

He rode down from that northern town
Claimed nothing for his fare
And when he got to parliament
No taxpayer shelled out there
No moat had he, no duck island
No subsidised spouse porn
He had a faith deep in his heart
The rest he held in scorn.

The bills incurred while in that place
He settled willingly.
For barrels, fuse and gunpowder
He asked no subsidy.
Let's raise a million pints of ale
And pop a million corks
To one so rare in parliament –
An honest man. Guy Fawkes.

2010

UNDAUNTED

9 November 1989:
Fall of the Berlin Wall.
9 November 2016:
'Election' of Donald Trump.
Cause and effect.
The ghastly end
to a chain of events
going back to the 80s.
Gorbachev's brave reforms.
Yeltsin's kleptocratic gangster-coup.
9/11. Gulf War.
Islamic State.
Brexit
and the rise of the populist Right.
This is a pivotal moment.
In the centenary year
of a Red revolution which shook the world
the Left needs to reclaim its heritage
and move forward.
Undaunted.
But in order to do so with clarity
we first have to look back.

Not right back to the beginning.
That path has been well-trodden
by thousands of writers
in millions of words:
the victories and the travesties,
the advances and the betrayals.
I'm going back just 28 years:
to February 1989 in East Berlin.
I was there.
On my four tours of the GDR
between 1986 and 1989
I had watched the East German Left

organize to growing effect
against the fossilized Party leadership
and now, inspired by Gorbachev's Soviet reforms,
they were openly demanding change.
More democracy.
More socialism.
(I'll never forget the banners:
'Mehr Sozialismus, bitte!')
Of course things couldn't stay the same.
Gorbachev was right to do what he did.
But he was betrayed.
The good went out with the bad.
The baby with the bathwater.
And the people paid the price.

The Wall fell.
The brave activists of the Left
who brought it down
were swamped by hordes
blinded by Bild Zeitung,
fighting over bananas.
Across Eastern Europe
worlds collapsed overnight.
People celebrated.
In many ways they were right to.
Party by all means, we shouted –
but organize as well.
Take control of your own destinies.
Don't believe the lies of the West.
They promise you exotic travel
but you will have no money to travel
They promise exotic cars
but you will have no money for cars
They will destroy your industries
privatize your futures
and make you paupers in your own lands.
But too few listened.

Heart On My Sleeve

The cold, cruel masters
of a new world smiled.
It's the end of history, they said.
Socialism has failed
the red banner has fallen
and now, workers, we are your masters,
all over the world.

We'll close down. Sack. Downsize. Relocate.
Ship in cheap labour. Outsource. Bring in robots.
Force down wages.
Crush your spirit.
Cast you aside
secure in the knowledge that your champions are dead
and that our pet media mouthpieces
can save us from your wrath
by blaming your fate on others:
immigrants, refugees
and your sacked co-workers
now recast as your enemies -
as scroungers off your taxes.
Slowly the vice tightened:
slowly the penny dropped.
Twenty years on from the fall of the Wall
opinion polls stated
that a majority all over Eastern Europe
(not the liberal elites of course,
laughing into their lattes,
but the forgotten masses
ignored by the world's media)
believed that their lives were better before 1989.
That what was allowed to go into their mouths
mattered at least as much
as what was allowed to come out of them.
That without economic democracy -
without jobs, healthcare, education, housing -
political democracy was meaningless

and that globalization, free trade
and neo-liberalism
were the enemies of working people everywhere,
East and West.
But the mass Red parties of the European Left
had disappeared in a welter of spineless apology
and self-loathing
leaving an open goal
for the populists of the Right.

And now
while we argue amongst ourselves
it is the likes of Trump, Le Pen and Wilders
who try to steal our clothes -
who use weasel words
to spread the politics of hate.

Elsewhere in the world
the modern secular movements
for liberation and education
slowly collapsed without their Soviet mentors,
leaving a void.
A people still oppressed and poor
searched for their own champions,
their own protectors.
Enter the fundamentalists.
For Trump and Le Pen
read ISIS and the Taliban:
the same weasel words,
the same dead-end reality –
literally so
for those young, duped jihadis.

So where do we go from here?
One thing is for sure.
Now as then
the choice is clear.

Heart On My Sleeve

Socialism or barbarism.
We must reclaim
the territory which the populists have stolen.
This is the challenge.
A hundred years on
from the great stand in Russia
Let's make another stand.
A modern stand.
A stand against globalization and neoliberalism.
Against nationalism and division.
Against racism and homophobia.
Against fundamentalism and misogyny.

Undaunted.

A LOAD OF BELLOC'S

Hilaire Belloc's 'Cautionary Tales', 'Bad Child's Book of Beasts' and 'More Beasts for Worse Children' were my earliest poetic inspirations aged about seven. Later in life I wrote some of my own.

A CAUTIONARY TALE
Being the Story of Steven, who became a Music Journalist, and was Cut Off in his Prime.

Young Steven was a Clever Thing –
He used to Play, and Dance, and Sing
And cut up Worms, and smash up Chairs
And push Old Ladies down the Stairs
And as he grew he got so bold
He'd never do as he was told
And Ma and Pa got rather riled
About their Sordid Little Child.
But, following his Teenage Years,
And Spots, and all the Normal Fears,
Young Steven formed a Clever Plan
To make himself a Famous Man.
He tried the Stage, but, sad to say
The Crowds told him to go away
So he - a normal recourse, this -
Became a Music Journalist.
Before too long young Steven's Fame
Was such that mention of his Name
Would bring Huge Gasps of Admiration
From every Corner of the nation!
His articles (this made him proud)
Were often praised, and Read out Loud
As Prime Examples of the Art
Of Careful Writing from the Heart.
His work won Prizes, and Awards
And Boat Trips on the Norfolk Broads
And soon young Steven was the Toast
Of Decent Folk from Coast to Coast.
But with this Adulation came
(A consequence of Wealth and Fame)

The Bold Attentions of a Crowd
Of Wicked Persons, Wild and Loud!
These Persons of Appalling Taste
Made after Steve in Fearful Haste
And pinned our Hero to the Floor –
Then had their way, twelve hours or more.
And then some Sheep, some Rats and Mice
And Other Creatures Not So Nice
Made Lustful Concourse with our Steve
And did things no-one would believe.
Things, sad to say, he did enjoy –
The Nasty and Perverted Boy.

Next morning, Steven woke in pain
And yelled for help – but all in vain
Then he gazed down in shocked surprise
At the Sad Sight which met his Eyes.
A Sore large as a Human Ear
On Steven's Member did appear
And, sad to say, it grew and grew
(As Sores so very often do.)
The Doctor came, and shook his Head
And filled Our Hero's Heart with dread –
A Portent of an Awful Fate;
'Yes, we will have to amputate.'
Now Steven's Pride and Joy is gone!
He sadly walks the streets alone
With but a Stump, inflamed and gory.
Here I shall end his tragic story.

The Moral of this tale is clear..
If young and male, go drink some Beer
Write Poetry (even if it's rank)
Hold Pickets outside Barclays Bank
Buy Morrissey LPs, eat Grass
Do Good Things for the Working Class
Go Trainspotting or take up Chess –
But don't write for the Music Press!

1988. (For me Morrissey was always an idiot, but he's turned out to be an even bigger one than I thought)

THE MAGGOT

The Maggot's not for Recipes, at least that's my advice.
It's true that he looks rather like a wriggly grain of Rice
But don't use him in Puddings, don't serve him up with Curry
For if you do, your Dinner Guests will leave in quite a Hurry…
He's best for catching Barbel, Dace, Perch, Gudgeon, Bream and Bleak.
(To make him wriggle when it's cold, just warm him in your Cheek.)
His Pupa's called a Caster, and is used for Castor Oil*
That's why it tastes revolting and makes Small Children recoil.
And, after several days as Caster, turns into a Fly.
(An insect you'll find on neglected Pets after they die.)
So if you don't like the Maggot, I have only this to say.
Just make sure that the Children feed the Hamster EVERY day…

*this may actually not be true

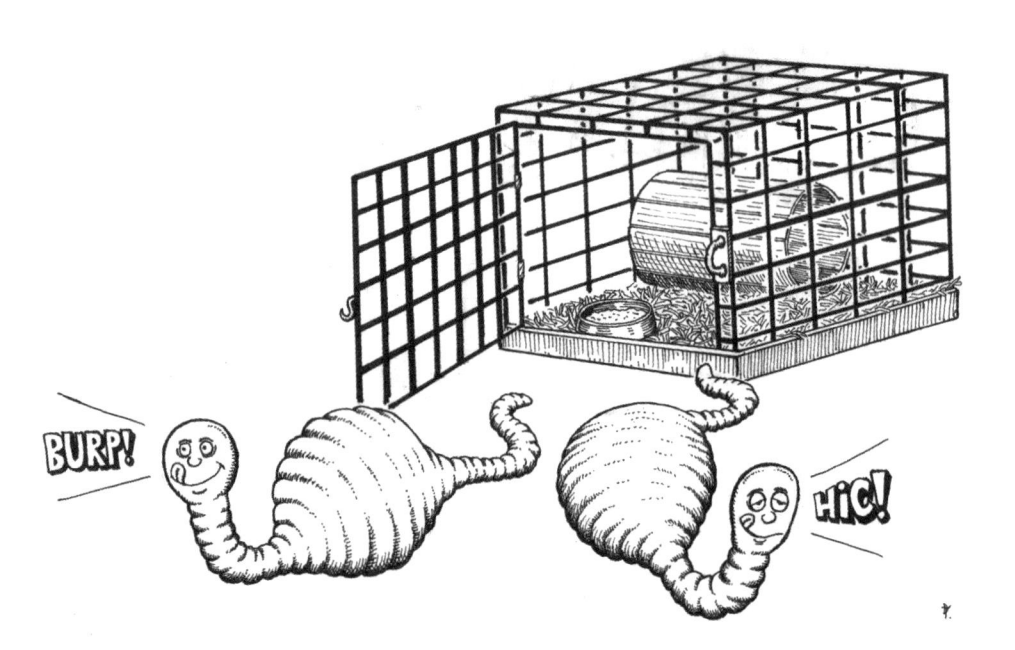

1996

THE BRITISH BULLFROG

Six inch sperm in garden centre
Strange, zygotic waggle dance
Disembodied, black placenta
Hitched a ride on foreign plants.
Uninvited and unwanted.
Poet says 'I'll take them home!'
Four enormous bullfrog tadpoles
In my pond and free to roam.

Press release from the Home Office:
It's a witch hunt, there's no doubt.
'Catch these immigrant amphibians!
They're illegal – stamp them out!
They'll wipe out our native species!'
(Don't tell me: they're weird, they smell,
Nick our jobs and shag our pond life
And they're on the dole as well.)

Crashing down, the eco-jackboot.
'No, they can't stay in your pond!
You'll be fined at least a thousand
If you let these things abscond!'
Semen-like, they squirm in protest.
'Freedom for the Southwick 4!'
But I know the awful verdict:
Custody for evermore.

 Few months in an old aquarium
Then this macro-spunk grows legs
Diet of red meat and chicken –
Turn their snouts up at ants' eggs…
One year more and they are sorted.
Saved from eco-Tory doom.
Summer: big pit in the garden.
Winter: in our living room.

Now their diet is worms and crickets
(Big worms and big crickets, sure.)
Grow two inches every year
And we love them – sod the law!
Soon they'll want some bigger victims
And the poet has a plan
Vengeance on the great oppressor
From our huge pit bullfrog clan...

Cats kill frogs – I've seen them do it
As a kid that lesson learned
Saw the corpse and shook with anger -
Soon the tables will be turned!
Pampered Kitty meets the posse.
Bullfrogs think 'Mmm..nice and fat
One rich owner – what's the flavour?
Yes! Our favourite! Kit-E-Kat!'

Feline diet makes them bigger
Hungrier and sharper still
Militant amphibian army
Huge of mouth and iron of will.
Tories, fascists, High Court judges
Down their throats the same old way
As they croak 'No deportations!
British Bullfrogs – here to stay!'

1996

Heart On My Sleeve

THE RAT-TAILED MAGGOT

I'm sure the Maggot makes you feel quite ill.
The Rat-tailed Maggot's more unsettling still!
You'll find him in a stagnant, foetid Pool
(A Cattle-trough's a good place as a rule)
Suspended upside down, his usual station
Feasting on Decomposing Vegetation
and breathing through a Membraneous Extension
which penetrates the water's surface tension.
When grown, our dear Protagonist pupates
(along with many thousands of his mates)
In dried-up hollows formed by Cattle Piss.
And then the Final Metamorphosis.
Insect so foul...
Alack! What's this I see?
A Drone Fly. Pretty. Like a stingless Bee.
Succumbed, I fear, to boring middle age.
But oh, what glory in the Larval Stage!

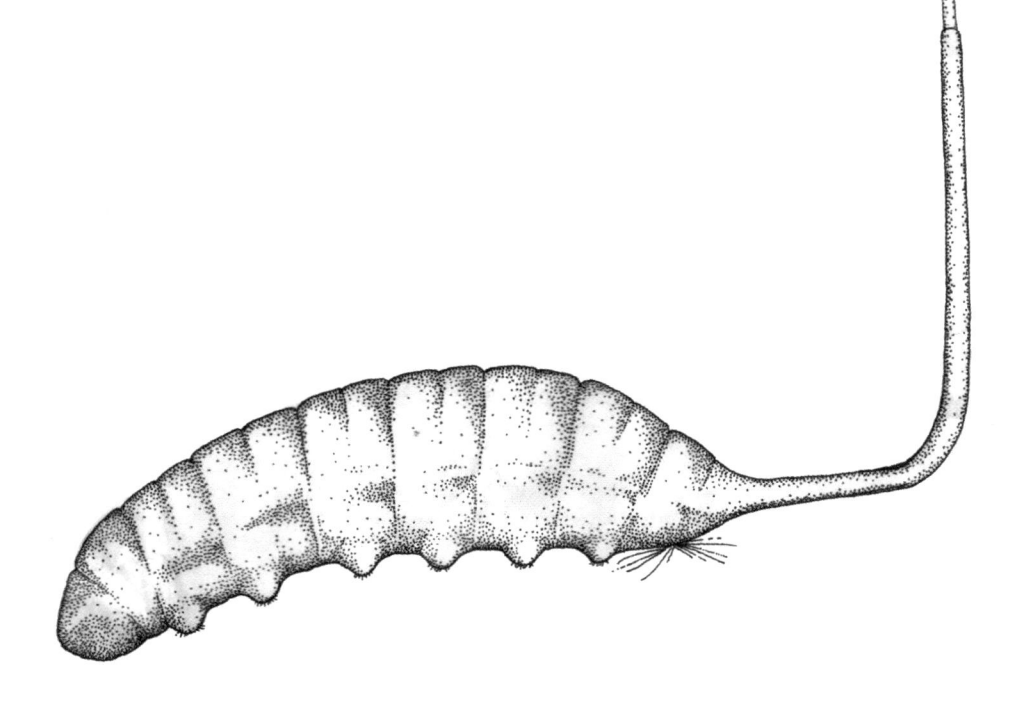

1996

HOW ARE YOUR BINS DOING IN THIS HOT WEATHER?
A question posed by local dutiful and hard-working Labour councillor Carl Walker on Facebook.

How are your bins doing in this hot weather?
Are the black sacks standing strong together?
Is your dustbin a sterile marvel…
Or have things got a little bit larval?

How are your bins doing in this hot weather?
Do they smell like Scottish gorse and heather?
Are they vessels you could wash a plate in…
Or are they gently pupating?

How are your bins doing in this hot weather?
Do they smell like camels' regions nether?
Or would you say 'They're fantastic –
No disco rice on my black plastic!'

How are your bins doing in this hot weather
Now you've cancelled that big get together
And you've thrown away all those faggots?
……………………………………………………………!

2020

THE CRAYFISH

I had a large blue Crayfish.
The Scots would call him 'bonnie.'
His tank was in my living room.
I called my crayfish Ronnie.

He had a spouse. Called Reggie.
He'd oft inseminate her.
Then one day something went amiss
And nasty Ronnie ate her.

And that's not all there was to it –
He ate his children too.
I found a Crayfish expert.
He said 'Crayfish often do'.

So Ronnie, brutal murderer
Was put in solitary
With plastic plants and nothing else
To keep him company.

The coward got his just deserts –
I bought an Axolotl.
As Axl prowled, so Ronnie cowered:
Yes, Ronnie lost his botl!

1996

THE AXOLOTL

The Axolotl is a beast unsung.
It stays a Larva. It's forever young.
If Nature ran its course, the Axolotl
Would be a Salamander. But it's notl.

1995

THE LUGWORM

If Male and, shall we say, Under-Endowed
And shrivelled yet still further by the Sea
The Lugworm is a beast to make you proud.
So dig one up: examine carefully
His Manly Shape, a full three inches long.
Thin at the bottom, thicker in the Gland.
A vulnerable Bell, and then a Hole.
He hangs, all damp and floppy, in your hand.
And now, perchance, think on the Angler's Hook
Which penetrates the Creature at the Tip.
'Enough!' you cry. You're right! I'll stop right there
As howls of protest rise beneath my Zip…

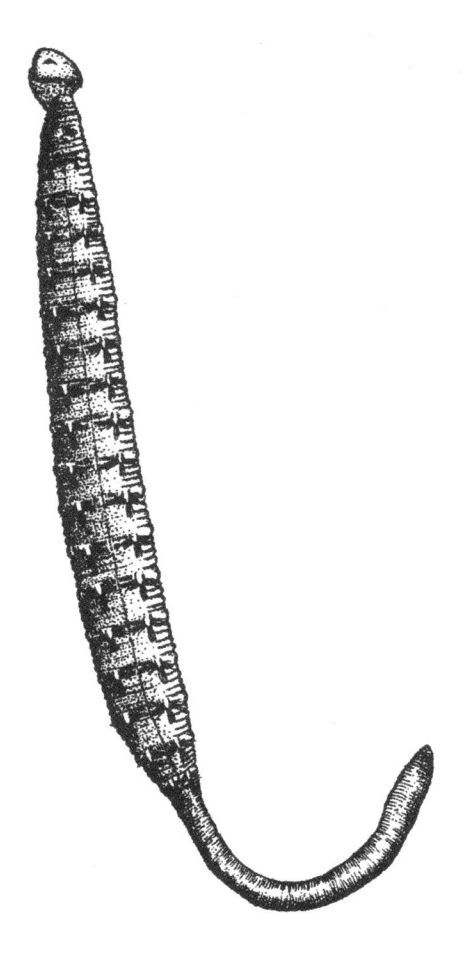

1996

THE SLUG

Mollusc for sure, but Aperitif? Non-starter.
Not the cachet of the Oyster, I regret.
In truth, my friend, you have few Redeeming Features
And even I do not want you as a Pet.
Time after time I will see friends' faces harden
As I approach with you nestling in my palm
When they insist that I throw you in the Garden
I will comply, although I wish you no harm.
Poor, homeless Snail. Pray, do you sell the Big Issue?
Ugly for sure, but you have efficient Glands.
Few Football Chairmen are actually this slimy...
Over the fence now! Time to wash my hands!

1996

THE LEMMING

The Lemming is the ultimate Commuter –
Same set-faced stare, same grey determination.
When Instinct says his final day has come
He sets off grimly for his Destination.
'Be quick!' says Mrs. Lemming, unaware
'I'm cooking you your favourite meal tonight'
The booking clerk asks 'Single or return?
Oh, sorry, single. You're a Lemming, right?
But hang on sir – they've got an offer on.
It's cheaper if you get a day return.
And my mate's mum's in the Samaritans…'
Such laudable, compassionate concern!
But we who clone our Sheep and Vegetables
Without so much as a remorse-filled Sniff
Will ne'er hold back that unseen, mighty Hand
That sends a Lemming to his final Cliff.

1996

(NB: I am aware that lemmings don't really jump off cliffs much.)

THE DON'T CARE BEAR

The Don't Care Bear's got purple hair
A padlock round his neck
His dad says 'That's no son of mine!'
His mum's a nervous wreck...
He lives on chips and Special Brew –
Not soppy stuff like Honey
You'll find him in the underpass –
(He'll ask you for some money)
He's got a mate called Tigger
And another one called Owl
They're in a band called 'PUNK'S NOT DEAD!'
They make the neighbours howl...
His parents named him Jeremy
His mates all call him Poo!
Says 'A.A. Milne's a knob-end, mate.
D'you want some Special Brew?'

1996

WRITTEN FROM SCRATCH

The Earth is in a right old mess -
We've screwed it up indeed.
Pollution, global warming
And endless corporate greed.
So many species threatened
And some already gone -
Our planet groans in anguish
While the juggernaut rolls on.

We worry about the elephants
The bears and tigers too
And if they're close to dying out
We breed them in a zoo.
It seems the only ones we save
Are big or have some hair
'Cos 70 frog species have gone
And no one seems to care.

Now, since a kid, I've always loved
the world which crawls and squirms
I've snakes and toads and newts at home
And even some pet worms….
And there's a special little mite
The same size as a flea
I've always had a soft spot for -
Though no, not literally.

Now some blame the Brazilians
And some blame good old soap -
One long established guest of ours
Is quickly losing hope.
For centuries it munched its fill
Oblivious to class -
As fond of pauper's privates
As a bit of Royal arse.

But in our hygiene-conscious age
It seems it's had its day:
Even the Goths and Palace fans
Are scrubbing it away.
And if we carry on like this
The verdict is succinct -
Our one time nether nemesis
Will soon become extinct!

This is for conservationists
Who stand for animal rights
You need to make a bit of space
In underpants and tights…
It's time to give it house room
And not just in your house
So heed the call of Nature now -
And save the pubic louse.

2013

VICTORIA ROAD
Every so often, the Tories call for a return to 'Victorian values...'

There was a Time, before the Car
(A Better Time, some say, by far)
When Queen Victoria's Scepter'd Arm
kept all her subjects safe from Harm
(as long as they were Rich, of course)
And folk were flogged without Remorse
for being Ill and being Poor
and eating Gruel and wanting More
and stealing Sheep, and bits of Food,
and worst of all, for being Rude…
A Nicer Folk there'd never been -
Their Lavatories were always clean
their well-scrubbed Kitchens bright and neat
and Table Legs veiled and discreet.
A people Thrifty, Kind, Correct,
and most importantly, Select.
I'm sure, Dear Reader, you will know
That this was Many Years ago
And such a State Pure and Sublime
bears no Resemblance to our Time
Where Impoliteness (sad to say)
and Indiscretion rule the day
Along with Sex, and Canine Turds,
And many different kinds of Words
Which to the folk of Former Times
Would have been Foul and Grievous Crimes!
Now in the Godless, Stinking Pit
In which we hapless Folk all sit
Enveloped in the Hellish Flames
of Techno Beats and Video Games
There are some folk whose Stated Ways
Hark right back to those far-off Days.
'Tis not the Etiquette they seek
To ape, neither the understated Chic,
But for Victoria Road they hanker.
Unfettered rule of Boss and Banker.

Cold Market Forces, shorn of Care.
The Iron Fist of Laissez Faire.
They start their Plan in Earliest School
Where Endless Testing is the rule
Subservience a Hallowed Grail
And Creativity past the Pale.
Their aim in this is very clear.
By means of Ignorance and Fear
they seek to turn the British Race
into a Folk who 'Know Their Place' -
Incapable of Sovereign Thought,
obsessed with Adverts, what they've Bought,
Celebrities, and Royal Poo.
The Drones in Milton Friedman's Zoo.
Hence their Curriculum so bland
Which no Decent Teacher can stand
Hence Admonitions Long and Stern
That what you Are is what you Earn
Hence, too, distrust of Roaming Minds
Creative Thinkers of all kinds
Called 'Chattering Classes' and thus scorned.
Oh, Albion, you have been warned!
Victoria Road is looming fast:
The die is very nearly cast.
Unthinkables are coming true.
Yes, one by one Bad Laws pushed through -
and met, not with a howl of Rage,
but Acquiescence, on the page
and on the street. Our Trusted Friends
now look to very different ends.
The Guardian? A Sychophant
Of power: emasculated, headless Ant.
The BBC moans on its knees
Undone by Tory appointees
and now a National Anaesthetic –
its dissident protests pathetic.
The TUC? A Satellite Dish.
A Vacant Stare, a long-dead Fish.
A Nation's Rebels? On a hike

To Game Shows, Adverts and the like.
A Foul Corruption stalks the land
And Opposition is so bland
That Boyzone's well-groomed Pubic Hair
Is Communistic by compare.
And worse to come. Portillo cites
The Poor, the Sick, now 'parasites'
And soon – the Workhouse?
Spiv-scum power.
Banana Britain's darkest hour.
A slavering, slobbering pig-dog Press
Laps up, laughs off each new Excess
A token slap, then back for more –
a Nation rotten to the core.
I'll rage until my rage takes fire
'Gainst each corrupt and bloated liar
I will not cease from Mental Fight
I spit upon their heartless Right
I vomit on the Twisted Code
which takes us down Victoria Road.

1995 - (though if you replace Portillo with Cummings, it could have been written yesterday)

'JOURNALISM'

THE BIBLE ACCORDING TO RUPERT MURDOCH
I wrote this after Murdoch's corporate tentacles enveloped William Collins - a publishing house which, among other things, produces the Bible. Based on his track record as a proprietor, here's the New Revised Version.

In the beginning was the Word, and the Word was Gotcha! And the Lord Rupert said let there be a Royal Family, and let enormous quantities of trivia and drivel be written about them, yea even unto the point where a mentally subnormal yak couldn't possibly find it interesting any more, and let babies be born unto this Royal Family, and let the huge swathes of sycophantic, nauseating sludge written about them surpass even that written about their parents, even though these babies and their parents are about as interesting as a wet afternoon on the terraces at Selhurst Park.

And the Lord Rupert said let there be soap operas, and let each of these soap operas be so mind-numbingly moronic as to make a wet afternoon at Selhurst Park seem a truly uplifting experience, and let entire forests and the ecological balance of several continents be destroyed in the endless vistas of retarded outpourings about these unspeakable transmissions.

And let there be enormous breasts, and endless bonking, and hours and days and weeks and months and years of chauvinistic right-wing propaganda so that the brain-dead prats who like the bonking and the soap operas and the breasts and the royal stories get the politics as well.

And let any journalist who tries to stand up to the proprietor and editor in the name of truth, and intelligence, and integrity, and journalistic standards, be summarily dismissed, and cast forever into a bottomless pit of decomposing chimpanzee smegma, and let those journalists who suffer this fate rejoice at the great career move they have just made.

And the Lord Rupert looked at his work, and even he saw that it was a load of crap, but this was the enterprise culture and it sold millions so it was good. And on the same basis he decided to take over the television too, and the earth itself wept, and little robins vomited, and cuddly furry animals threw themselves under trains, and the whole thing was filmed by Sky Channel for a horror nature programme, and the most awful thing of all was that this was just the beginning...

1989

A SUGARED DISH

Alan Sugar, Spurs chairman, was part of the Football Association team which did the deal giving Rupert Murdoch's Sky TV exclusive rights to broadcast Premiership football matches. At the time Sugar was chairman of Amstrad, one of the country's leading manufacturers of satellite dishes.

High in the sky the angler sits
in smug anticipation
No boundaries now hold back his dream
of global domination
Across the world his lines are cast
and now he lies in wait:
he's fishing for the human mind
and football is the bait.

The Premier League's a sugared dish
so swiftly, cleverly bought.
It's good bait, but he needs some more:
he buys up every sport.
The fish bite: he removes their guts
and leaves one single eye
fixed on the Sun, Sky News and Fox:
One folk, one state, one Sky.

The rich elite rake in the cash:
it only flows one way.
The small clubs teeter on the brink –
some pinstriped vulture's prey.
Developers eye up the grounds
whole lives are built upon
while Southerners in Man U shirts
switch televisions on.

The angler plays monopoly:
the government connives.
The shoals of fish gorge on the dish
which brightens up their lives
And Murdoch nears his final dream:
a global superstate
where minds are caught and minds are set
and football is the bait.

1992

DOMESTICITY

TWO GLASTONBURY ERRORS
Dedicated to the memory of Arabella Churchill

Now I've performed at Glastonbury since 1982 –
That's 26 so far I think, though each year feels like new
I've seen it grow from hippy roots into a massive splurge
You get the lot, from ranting poets to quids-in corporate dirge
And that's OK. Each to their own. We old school hardcore purists
And all the mobile-cashpoint-weekend-hippie Glasto tourists.
I have a thousand memories of sunshine, rain and flood!
Joe Strummer on the main stage, John Peel in the mud…
No time for all. Two special stories: they're a rare old mixture.
The beer-befuddled memoirs of a punk rock Glasto fixture.

The first concerns a gruesome and apocryphal event
Concerning those unfortunates ensconced in the Dance Tent
One afternoon when Glasto staff were cleaning out the loos.
The bloke inside the toilet truck had two buttons to choose –
The one emblazoned 'Suck' and the other labelled 'Blow'.
Wrong button, wrong place and wrong time. The end result?
Oh, no.

The second is more personal and close to home, I'd say.
My wife and I were wandering one sunny Saturday
Amidst the close-pressed masses of a modern Glasto crowd
When she had a whim to do something to make her husband proud
Give me a lift, despite my beers, and really set me up
So she gently reached behind herself to make a loving cup
But my stopping by the beer tent quite undid her wifely plan
And the loving cup was given to an unsuspecting man…
Her fingers knew at once the heinous nature of her error
And she dashed off in embarrassment, confusion, pain and terror!
I've never asked Robina if the grounds for her surprise
Were because her chosen target was over- or undersized…
Or was it just a different shape? Well, that's as it may be.
Long live Michel Eavis, and long live Glastonbury!

2001 (updated 2020)

A HOLE SERIES
...of poems for my wife

I love the whole of you.
And all the rest of you.
Not just a part of you.
I love your hole.
Clitorally speaking.
And that's the long, short and curly of it.

I have a hole in my heart.
I love you
Hole heartedly.

You're feeling tired and stressed.
I find the cure.
Holeistically.

In the bath
Our favourite meal -
Toed in the hole.

On tour.
What's this?
An envelope
in my mandola case.
'We love you'
it says on the outside.
And inside?
Short curly ones.
Long straight ones.

Now that's what I call
a holeogram!

For a holemeal
We love hole food.
Chocolate spread.
Ice cream.
Finger doughnuts.
But hole grain
is out!

Holesale?
Although rubbish,
on this point at least
the Beatles were right.
Money
can't
buy
you
love.

Driving through West Sussex.
Sign says: 'Crossbush - 1 mile'
Keep us away!
It's got to be a hell hole.
And I can't stand the thought of a holey war...

2000

ON BEING DEFROSTED

'It needs defrosting, love, and quickly too.
My husband bought it half an hour ago
Expecting that this lump of icebound flesh
would be our lunch – he hasn't got a clue.
I said it was a foolish thing to buy.
I told him that you have a microwave.
Shame-faced, he drove me over in the car.
It needs defrosting, love, and so do I!'

The chicken frozen, you all wet and hot.
It took a while – you, thirty seconds flat.
But still your wifely duties weren't ignored –
Your (ex) husband got dinner on the dot.
I'll buy our chickens fresh and cook for you
But yes, the recipe will stay the same
As on that Sunday morning lost in time.
While dinner's cooking, we'll be cooking too.

2002

A NASAL APPRAISAL
(For my Darling Wife, Xmas 2001)

I love your Nose
Your Nose I kiss
I know it's not
Your Clitoris
I love your Nose
It's on your Face
Your Clit is in
A Different Place
I love your Nose
I'm glad it's There
And not among
Your Pubic Hair
I love your Nose
Its Bogies Fine
And when you're Pissed
They taste of Wine!

I love your Nose
I say with Candour
I love its Splendour
I love its Grandeur
Here is the Truth
Without Conjecture
I love Your Nasal
Architecture!
Your Steel Eyes Shine
Your Nostrils Flare
I catch a glimpse
Of Nasal Hair
And When You Sneeze
I'm On My Knees...
I love your Nose!
I love your Nose!

Heart On My Sleeve

I love your Nose
Seat of my Lust
It's listed by
The National Trust
I love your Nose
It Fuels my Fire
A Sturdy Oak
A Mighty Spire
A Profile Fine
Chiselled in Stone
Face like a Queen
Nose like a Throne
And when it Bleeds
They know -
in Leeds...
I love your Nose!
I love your Nose!

THE SEETHING WELLS MEMORIAL SOCIAL SURREALIST SECTION

CORONAVIRUS VS THE TETLEY BITTERMEN

There was a sign. They did their best.
'The Charles Bronson Arms is shut.'
The Bittermen kicked down the door.
'Coronavirus can get fucked.
It's yellow and it tastes like piss.
There's nowt about it can inspire us.
There's none of that Corona here.
Bradford's the home of Tetleyvirus!'

The Bittermen supped twenty pints
And ate their weight in Radford's pies.
A toast to 'Boris' followed soon
Abuse for experts spreading lies
And when a few short weeks had passed
They paid the price for what they'd done.
The final score in Bradford town
Was Tetleys 0, Corona 1.

FROGSPAWN MAN VERSUS THE BOY RACERS

Mid nineties.
March.
West Sussex.
I've been to a stream
next to the A27
looking for frogspawn
to populate our brand new garden pond.
I guess I first went there when I was about seven
and have been many times since.
The road is much wider now
the cars are faster
and most of the stream is gone
but one stubborn bit remains
next to the concrete and the cars
and the frogs have obviously had
an orgy of Bacchanalian proportions.
I've found lots of spawn, very quickly.
A glutinous, black-specked mess
fills my bucket.
It's a beautiful spring day.
I'm very happy
full of memories of my father
seven years old again.
I stand by the side of the road
next to the traffic lights
and wait for my lift home.

Suddenly I realise
that an inarticulate-sounding man in his mid twenties
in some kind of penis extension car
has wound down his window
and is shouting abuse at me.
The lights change -
the glans glides off.
Then another man makes a two fingered gesture at me.
A car full of techno nerds
turns down the techno
and hurls a collective techno insult.
The next time the light goes red

a middle aged, middle class Southwick zip up jumper husband
in a middle aged, middle class Southwick zip up jumper car
draws up beside me
and glares at me with undisguised contempt.
He looks as though he would like to shout something
but no-one from Southwick talks to strangers
let alone shouts at them
so he just glares at me.

I stare back.
I don't glare.
I just stare.
I am very puzzled.

I check my person.
I am fully clothed.
My flies are done up.
My mud spattered T-shirt bears the logo
of an obscure folk band from Wigan.
Does everyone really hate the Tansads that much?

I am totally confused.
It's a beautiful Spring day
I am standing by the traffic lights
on a West Sussex A road
holding a bucket of frogspawn
and suddenly everybody hates me!
Another car hurtles past -
occupants screaming abuse.

Then the lights change again.
A car draws up beside me.
A very flash, shiny one.
The boy racer inside is shaking his head.
He is gesturing to me
as though I am about to do something totally unacceptable
to something very important to him
and he really doesn't want me to.
I stand there.
I gaze at him in absolute bewilderment.

Heart On My Sleeve

His window opens.
Then his mouth.
'Bloody squeegee merchant. Don't you touch my fucking car. Piss off and get a fucking job!'

I look at him in astonishment.
What has he just said?

Then I realise.
I am standing by the traffic lights.
I am holding a bucket.
He thinks I am about to start cleaning his car windscreen without his permission.

I walk over to the car.
I tip the bucket up slightly
and proffer the contents to him.
It is his turn to be confused.
He's a boy racer.
His car has a Romford dealership sticker on the window.
He doesn't exactly have a herpetologist's soul.
He stares at the contents of my bucket.
He doesn't know what it is.
However, I think he realises that I'm not going to start cleaning his windscreen with it.

The lights change
he roars off
I walk back to the side of the road
and laugh till the tears run down my cheeks,
till my sides are killing me
till I pull a muscle.

It's March
eight years later.
Our pond is full of spawn -
the grandtadpoles of that original bucketful.
As I crouch to look at the developing specks
the memory comes back.
I start to shake

the tears run down my cheeks
I nearly overbalance into the pond.
I run inside
I write this poem
I feel so happy.

2004

BEER GARDENING
(for all at the Evening Star, Surrey Street, Brighton)

Come into the Beer Garden!
It's not very far.
What's that light that points the way?
It's the Evening Star.
We all love Beer Gardening
As the sun goes down.
Who's that crashed out on the floor?
InCapability Brown.

Come into the Beer Garden
Through the Golden Gate!
Sunburst makes your Hophead swim -
Meltdown seals your fate...
Peas, then Leeks, then Sycamore.
Got to let it go!
What's that in the Yucca Plant?
You don't want to know....

Four hours in the Beer Garden -
God, I need a kip.
Insects are all outsects now.
Flies have got no zip.
Stagger onto the last train.
Cuddle up in bed.
Red Hot Poker's lost his poke.
Shrimp Plant's there instead.

2006

DESIGNATED AREAS
I originally wrote this during the Yugoslav civil war in the mid-90s.
It has been updated for this 40 year anthology of my work, but its core images remain.
It's inspired by and dedicated to the Slovenian social surrealist collective, Laibach.

I know this doesn't sound very poetic
since poets are often portrayed as
miserable self-pitying wrecks
but nearly every morning
I wake up feeling really good.
I'm sixty-two years old
and the only time I have ever had
'a proper job'
was for eleven months
forty years ago.
I'm a poet
I can earn a living as a poet
and I get to travel all over the world.
I love writing
I love the world
and I love to travel
so there isn't much of a problem.
I do look forward to coming home though.
Most of all, I miss my wife.
I love her very much.
I miss her more and more as the years go by.
I miss a decent pint of real ale.
I miss my football team
and my pet corn snakes Napoleon and Emma
and although this may seem incongruous
for an angry punk poet
I miss our garden.
I love gardening.
I'm a new wave gardener.
I love planting things and watching them grow.
I love the feeling of being close to the sea
and close to the soil.
But there's another side to all this.
There are things which turn me into a total horticultural psychopath.

A ruthless agricultural megalomaniac.
And not just me – all red-blooded gardeners
feel the same.
I'll tell you what they are:
WEEDS.

Now some woolly-minded liberal do-gooders
will tell you
that weeds
are just
'flowers growing in the wrong place.'
But I know better.
Weeds are scum.
Weeds are genetically impure renegades
freeloading on my carefully distributed
ecologically sound fertilizer
they have no right to exist
and they must DIE.
Or at the very least
KNOW THEIR PLACE.
Let them clog up railway sidings
and annoy the trainspotters
or eke out their miserable existences
on motorway central reservations
deprived of nutriments
and blasted by lead fumes.
These are their designated areas.
Now I'm not being excessive:
my resettlement plan
for these anarchistic subvegetables
is approved by the United Nations
and I have a peacekeeping compost heap
in place at all times
but whatever I try
whatever awesome penalties I introduce
however many black bin liners I fill
the weeds keep coming
and when I am away
- on tour, abroad, whatever –

they regroup
organize a morale-boosting press conference
with the stinging nettles
in the overgrown alley
at the other side of the fence
and creep back.
Bindweed is the worst.
Bindweed really brings out the Chetnik in me.
A final solution for bindweed
- that's what I want.
I have a Zen Stalinist five year plan
for my little harbourside
agricultural co-operative
and bindweed
chickweed
thistles
and crappy strands of stray grass
are not part of it.
And I'm sure any gardeners reading this
will agree with me.
I'm sure you don't like weeds
any more than I do.
I'm sure you've all turned your back gardens
into horticulturally pure areas, haven't you?
Ethnic cleansing.
Now there's a concept.

OH FOR THE DAYS WHEN 'SPAM' WAS JUST A MONTY PYTHON SKETCH

Thanks to the internet
my wife is a very happy woman.
My penis is now forty-seven feet long
it stays erect for weeks at a time
and is garlanded by hundreds of genuine Rolex watches
acquired with the millions I have won
in various Albanian lotteries
and the billions generously deposited in my accounts
by the grateful executors of the wills
of innumerable African tribal chiefs
all mysteriously deceased
along with their entire extended families
in improbably gruesome lawnmower accidents in Liechtenstein.
My account with Lloyds has been suspended.
(I don't have one.)
My wife's breasts
enlarge and reduce, spontaneously,
as we use our 95% discounted software
to gaze at the pictures of our free timeshare apartments
enjoying continuous multiple orgasms
whilst admiring our genuine Chinese historical artefacts
purchased online from Hong Kong.
Our garden is full of imported rubber.
Not rubber sex toys
or even rubber boots
just: rubber.
I have more free Coldplay MP3s
than you could wave a suicide note at.
I also have Kate Moss Suction Power.
I don't know what that is,
but I am hoping it may be useful
next time the toilet needs unblocking.
I now know the Cyrillic alphabet
and the Polish for
'I've gained an inch and a half so far!'

Heart On My Sleeve

Every morning, a new surrealist word juxtaposition appears in my inbox
as the spammers seek to avoid the filter.
Applicator fornicate!
Crabmeat be Paris!
Gash ineptitude!
Out evoke in robins!
Consonant clitoris!
Bestiality service charge!
Decomposing lark's vomit engulf Crystal Palace!
(OK, I mad the last one up,
but the others are all genuine.)
And, to prove that truth is indeed stranger than fiction
in our brave new world,
my website is recommended
as one of the top fifty stockbroking sites
on many search engines.

Now that really IS Pythonesque.

2007

NORTH KOREA MOURNS COMRADE MICKEY FINN OF T.REX

Mickey Finn, Marc Bolan's bongo playing sidekick in the mighty T.Rex, sadly died on January 12, 2003, at the age of 56. This sad event was, totally unjustly in my view, more or less ignored in the UK: sure, Mickey couldn't sing or play the bongoes very well, but he looked good on stage and was very much a part of T.Rex. However, his passing was very much mourned elsewhere. Many former UK rock legends, forgotten in their own country, have huge followings in Japan and other countries of the Far East, and although this is not common knowledge, Mickey Finn had his own Far Eastern following... though his was rather different. This is the text of a communique issued shortly after the news broke.

It is with unfathomable sadness and regret that the Dear Leader, Comrade Kim Jong Il, the Central Committee of the Korean Workers' Party, the regional organisations, the progressive women and youth and all the labouring masses throughout the Democratic People's Republic of Korea learned of the death of Comrade Mickey Finn, much-loved bongo player with T.Rex and beloved bongo teacher and percussive mentor to the revolutionary people of our Republic.

When the unbearable news of Comrade Mickey's untimely death reached the ears of the Korean people, spontaneous mass demonstrations broke out all over the homeland. Millions of workers, peasants and intellectuals immediately took to the streets in a huge show of proletarian love for Comrade Mickey, and the sound of bongoes being played slightly out of time rang out across all corners of the Republic. Above this occasionally erratic percussive clamour could clearly be heard the progressive slogans spontaneously rising from the lips of the people:

Glory to the immortal memory of Comrade Mickey Finn of T.Rex, through his much-loved recordings beloved bongo-playing tutor to Comrade Kim Il Sung, the Great Leader and his son Comrade Kim Jong-Il, the Dear Leader!

Long live the revolutionary and percussive Juche spirit embodied and reflected in the sound of Comrade Mickey's bongoes!

Death to the American imperialists and their British lackeys who dare to issue threats against the progressive and revolutionary nuclear weapons programme of the DPRK and conspire to spread lies about the homeland! Death to their filthy media running dogs who ignore the life and work of Comrade Mickey Finn!

Glory to his bongoes! Glory to authentically produced percussive sound! Death to electronically-produced and computer-generated so called 'dance music!' Let us take new initiatives in the field of culture to honour the memory of Comrade Mickey!

Let us make it clear to the progressive peoples of the world that 'house music' lives in the house of the bourgeoisie, and 'trance' is the state of mind of those who have been fooled by the lies of the U.S imperialists and their lackeys!

Let us ensure that henceforth the only 'techno' in revolutionary Korea is the ever greater technological development of our militant and steel-like response to all aggressors:

PEOPLE'S REVOLUTIONARY NUCLEAR WAR!

That the only 'deep house'
is the radiation-proof underground bunker of the Dear Leader,
Comrade Kim Jong-Il!

That the only 'garage'
is the silo system housing the launchers for our militant revolutionary
people's inter-continental nuclear ballistic missiles!

That the only 'acid house'
is the interrogation chamber reserved for all internal anti-Party elements!

That the only 'chill-out zone'
is the mortuary, destination of all those who dare to raise their hands against the revolutionary Korean people!

That 'Old Skool'
means but one thing -
the immortal teachings of Marx, Engels, Lenin....

AND STALIN!

Glory to the immortal memory of Comrade Mickey Finn!

(communique ends)

668: NEIGHBOUR OF THE BEAST

He's an interesting fellow:
yes, I must give him his due.
Goats out in the garden
Goblins in the loo
No Jehovah's Witnesses
Never sees a priest
Party wall is rather warm.
Neighbour of the beast.

The Goth at number 667
always gets my post
He lives across the road of course.
(With two bats and a ghost.)
The postman never gets it right.
I tell him 'Listen, mate:
It's Satanist suburbia –
I live at 668!'

He's a devil in the kitchen
Watch those speculators fry!
There's severed cocktail sausages
with home made nipple pie
Tagliatelle made from tapeworms
from dogs recently deceased
and the barbecue never goes out:
Neighbour of the beast.

He's got a little waiting list
of folk he wants to see
for a special dinner party
lasting all eternity…
On the menu: Ian Paisley,
Selwyn Gummer and the Pope.
For dessert: baked ayatollah.
Enter here – abandon hope!

1994

THE SACK
Dedicated to Tony Wright, front man of a wonderful Barnsley band called The Hurriers.

Twas 2am when I got back.
Morning Star party – brilliant craic.
I was dog-tired, the night pitch-black.
I reached behind for the rucksack
I'd left on the back seat. Alack!
There was a lack of rucksack black!
I nearly had a heart attack.
My mind went straight into flashback.
To Manette Street it did backtrack.
In Soho I the car did pack:
I'd left it in the road. Oh, cack…
Strange fingers would invade my sack
The contents heartlessly unpack -
My stuff I never would get back.
Oh awful day! Alas, alack!
Had it just held a mouldy snack
Perhaps a dirty anorak
Some Prozac in a blister pack
An empty bottle of cognac
Or gel for fighting dental plaque
A picture of Chateau Du Lac
Or even of the Merrimac
CD of Stan Webb's Chicken Shack
Some fixtures for a luggage rack
Biography of Jacques Chirac
(In hardback or in paperback)
A DVD of Crackerjack
A photo of Jiri Skalak
(too crap for Brighton's new attack)
an old, half-eaten Caramac
or other replaceable cack
The future would not seem so black.
It wouldn't class as a setback -
I'd just have bought a new rucksack.

But oh no. Cue the Goth soundtrack.
Inside that sack was my new Mac!
And on that new Mac I keep track
Of work, of life. I'm on the rack.
More precious than a Cadillac.
It's like a second scrotal sac...
And there is more. I'd just come back
From four good gigs, and all the stack
Of dosh I'd earned was in that sack -
And now I'd never get it back.
But then of light I spied a crack
For Tony Wright I'd driven back
From that great gig with that great craic.
Had he walked off with my rucksack?
But all my hopes I soon knocked back.
Like Amy, I went back to black.
'He's got more brains than a dead yak
Or a retarded stickleback
He's not a kleptomaniac!'
Or so I thought...
I hit the sack.
I slept like an insomniac
With thoughts of passwords folk could crack
With info found on my new Mac
And all that dosh they'd spend on smack.
And then I got a message back.
'Reet sorry, lad, I took tha sack.
I was so pissed… Come, get it back!'

My wife says Tony needs a whack.
A smack. A thwack upon the back.
She'd slept beside a maniac.
A panicking insomniac.
A Yorkshireman had pinched my sack -
And now, thank fuck, I've got it back.
So please, folks, give him lots of flack.
He gets this poem as payback!

2015

Heart On My Sleeve

FUGAZI, CLIFF RICHARD & ME

Lance Armstrong –
Banned from his sport
for taking performance enhancing substances.
A chemistry experiment on wheels.
The latest of many:
pilloried, infamous, cast out
while we invariably wonder how many of the others
dutifully joining in the chorus of condemnation
are whizzing around on a saddle
zooming around the track
or hoovering up the yards in the pool.
It got me thinking, though.
In sport, the worst thing you can do
is take drugs.
If you're caught
you become a non person
your achievements
however glorious
are immediately discounted
and wiped from the record books
and you are fated to live out your days
in a mixture of ignominy and obscurity.
Think what would happen
if the same principle was applied to rock n roll –
if every song
every album
every gig
performed by people who had taken drugs
was eradicated from the musical canon
and cast into the pit of oblivion.
It'd make Stalin's purges
Look like open mic night at an anarchist squat.
Carnage!
All my heroes – gone.
The Velvet Underground.

Heart On My Sleeve

Marc Bolan.
Dexys Midnight Runners.
The drug stabbing Clash.
All your heroes gone too.
The Grateful Dead?
Hendrix?
Acid house?
Reggae?
No more heroes any more!
I'd be safe though.
I got through my formative poetic years on beer
rather than the likes of LSD
which fortunately means
that my work has always been devoid of hippy bollocks
and when I talk about 'cherry blossom' I invariably mean boot polish.
Furthermore, Dark Star Six Hop Ale
is definitely NOT performance enhancing
in any sense of the word.
Is it, audience? Is it, darling?
No, I thought not.
But I am glad
that the worlds of sport and music have different rules
because I think I could scarcely bear to live in a world
where the only sounds to be heard
were those of Fugazi,
Cliff Richard
and me.

2013

THE SOCIAL SURREALIST WEAPONS INSPECTOR'S REPORT

I am one of a team
of social surrealist weapons inspectors
currently travelling through the United Kingdom
under very difficult conditions
searching for weapons of mass distraction.
The government
have denied that they exist
or have ever existed
or indeed that there is or could ever have been any reason
for New Labour to seek to distract the masses in the first place
and they have compiled an extensive dossier
of long-abandoned Labour Party achievements
as proof of their honesty, good intentions and political credibility.
These include:
creating a temporary Welfare State
nationalising the mines and railways
for a few years
reducing working hours and increasing workers' wages
a bit
and opposing the worst excesses of capitalism
from time to time
for a couple of months
in 1954
as long as it was alright with the CBI.
But a cursory glance round Britain
has uncovered hundreds of such weapons of mass destruction -
Big Brother
Pop Idol
endless meaningless 'celebrities'
The Sun 'newspaper'
and the Royal Family
to name but a few -
and our demands that they should be destroyed
in order to combat national supine gullibility
have met with strenuous opposition
not just from the government

but from a substantial number of private individuals
who scream incoherent and violent abuse
at anybody who seeks to remove these weapons
unquestioningly accept their lot
as part of the least healthy, worst educated and worst paid population
in Western Europe
and energetically defend their right to be exploited and lied to
by abject American government stooges
masquerading as the British Labour Party.

This proves not just the existence
but the supreme effectiveness
of the weapons of mass distraction
currently being employed by Mr Brown and his cronies.
We demand immediate action by the United Nations
in the form of strict sanctions
on fifth rate, lowest common denominator television programmes
and newspapers
and especially on the use of the phrase 'politically correct'
to attack anyone who isn't a right wing
misogynistic
bigoted
cretin
with the reflective powers of a lobotomised stoat.
We are, of course, working for British Intelligence -
we don't think there's enough of it about.

2003

THE MANDELSON VIOLIN CONCERTO

I'm the conductor
That means I'm in charge.
I know you loathe me.
Don't B sharp
or you'll end up flat.
Yes, I know the other lot
played that piece solidly
for eighteen years
but Terry Wogan likes it
so we've made it our theme tune.
It's not why you joined the orchestra?
You've been here 30 years?
Tough.
Yes, I know it's supermarket muzak
- all majors, no miners –
but it certainly strikes a chord.
Did you read that great review in the Daily Mail?
Play along,
Smile, sweetly,
or you're out of the orchestra.
If you want the Red Flag
join the SWP.
We're the Mike Flowers Pops.

1997

THE ZEN STALINIST MANIFESTO

Playing golf or being otherwise dull
with malice aforethought
watching TV for more than ten hours a week
discussing soap operas
(or any TV programmes or adverts
in the case of a stand-up comedian on stage)
and becoming obsessed with the work of
Quentin Tarantino
Damien Hirst
or William Burroughs
will become a criminal offence
punishable by five years' enforced participation
in a non-stop mime
juggling
and face painting workshop
in Slough.

The Berlin Wall will be rebuilt -
only five metres higher.
It will keep people out.
People like the World Bank
the International Monetary Fund
the Spice Girls
Price Waterhouse
Goldman Sachs
Jeffrey Archer
William Archer
Peter Mandelson
Helmut Kohl
and Boris Yeltsin.

Peter Lilley and Michael Portillo
will suffer immediate retrospective abortion.

In order to combat the increasing danger
to civilised society
posed by pig-ignorant

misogynistic
right-wing
testosterone-poisoned
road rage specialists
theme gulags will be introduced
for anyone who drives a van with scratches down the side
and shouts at or otherwise intimidates
lone women drivers at roundabouts
or buys shares in industries
which belonged to him in the first place.

These gulags will all be situated on Rockall
and will have three themes:
Saturday night in August on the Costa Del Sol
auction day at the used car emporium on Shoreham seafront
and happy hour in a Harlow theme pub.
All themes will run 24 hours a day
365 days a year
and inmates will be able to nominate their chosen
theme on arrival.
No theme changing will be allowed
but Clash albums
chess sets
and copies of 'The Ragged-Trousered Philanthropists'
will be available for rehabilitation purposes.

Tight security will be enforced.
Theme gulags will be surrounded by large, deep moats
filled with soya milk and real ale
guarded by pitbullfrogs
and kept under constant surveillance
by hundreds of high court judges
watching from carefully constructed ivory towers.

Boris Yeltsin will finally be recognised
as the traitor and Judas he is
and made to spend the rest of his days
cleaning out the toilets
at the Glastonbury Festival.
With his tongue.

Every Western government leader
and the entire staff of the United Nations
will be forced to walk naked
through the burnt-out towns
and mass graves
in what used to be the Socialist Federation of Yugoslavia
and then have the words
'Marshall Tito was right'
tattooed on their foreheads.

A Zen Stalinist National Curriculum
will be introduced into schools.
Albanian
- both dialects, Gheg and Tosk -
will become compulsory as a foreign language.
Reading Geoffrey Archer
and supporting Crystal Palace
will become not just highly illegal
but indicative of a disturbed mental state
requiring instant frontal lobotomy.

The Alarm will reform.
All school students will have to attend morning assembly
and sing the new National Anthem:
'68 Guns' by The Alarm.
Mike Peters of The Alarm
will become the new Welsh football manager
with David Icke as his assistant.

The Royal Family
will be allowed to remain as figureheads
but will have to join The Alarm.
Billy Bragg will become next in line to the throne
and rhythm guitarist in The Alarm.
All game show hosts
and everyone who works for the Sun
and the Times Literary Supplement
will be shot.
Their executions will be videoed

an acid house soundtrack will be added
and huge week-long parties
known as 'graves'
will begin.

Ken Livingstone and his pet newt Dennis
will become Prime Minister
and Chancellor of the Exchequer.
All privatised industries will be renationalised
without compensation
and a huge TV and poster campaign will be launched
saying simply
'Tell Sid tough shit.'
The Queen will be privatised
and promoted to lead singer of The Alarm.
The first Zen Stalinist Five Year Plan
will be published
declaring world peace and social surrealism
and the dark nightmare of monetarist madness
will finally come to an end.
For ever.

1995

SHORT & SWEET

THE MARXIST TOMATO GROWER

He sits
and waits
for his world
to turn red.
He knows it will,
eventually,
but it's taking
a hell of a long time.

THIS MEANS WAUGH

Auberon Waugh
is a terrible baugh.
But I'd still much rather
him than his father.

ROGERED! (an affectionate poke)
'Let me die a youngman's death' (Roger McGough)

Oh Roger, Roger, OBE
For services to poetry!
Touched by the Empire's latest breath
You'll never die a youngman's death…
A twilight in a health resort
A nursing home, and a fine port.
And, at the end, an epitaph
In Dailies Mail and Telegraph!

THE ULTIMATE FESTIVAL TOILET

Flushing Meadow, wild and free.
What a place for Glastonbury…
Hail the great hygienic plain.
Do the gig – then pull the chain!

SAYING GOODBYE

VERONICA

Veronica was one of the best:
a strong, independent, resourceful woman
perceptive, sensual and humanist, with a bullshit detector
so finely developed
you knew you couldn't get away with anything.
She was a fulcrum for her children
a rock of support for her friends
and inspired love and respect in everyone she met.
We talked about everything
far into the night
and when her cancer returned
and she began fighting it with the same zest for life
determination and optimism
which imbued everything she did
we talked about that too –
the really important things
the fundamentals of existence.
She went unbowed through the operations and tests
and even when in terrible pain
she had time for us, for our lives
our concerns, our feelings
dispensing opinions and advice
just as she had always done.
We always knew she was popular
but not until September
when we gathered at the crematorium
did we realise just how many people loved her.
The place was as packed
as the Square in Harlow
on the night Carter did their secret gig there.
It was like the North Stand
when Brighton played Liverpool in the 80s.
Most people were trying to be cheerful
we always knew she wouldn't have wanted it
any other way

her kids were smiling bravely through their tears
- and then it began.

Oh, Veronica!
In your lust for life
it was clear that right until the very end
you didn't believe it would happen this soon.
Death was the last thing on your mind.
You wanted to live
and so thoughts of your funeral
how you would have wanted it to be
would never even have occurred to you.
I guess your kids, numb with grief
and your amiably unassuming ex-husband
wanted to make things as easy as possible
and just went along with some distant family tradition.
I never even knew you had a Catholic background.
On the few occasions we discussed religion
'the afterlife'
and associated topics
our views coincided completely, or so it seemed to me –
and this after the black hand had already
made its presence felt.
Maybe it wouldn't have bothered you
that the final celebration of your life was turned into a travesty.
Perhaps, and totally in character, you'd have said
'I'll be dead, won't I? What will I care?'
But, in truth, I think it would have angered you
as it angered us.
Realising what was coming, we shifted uneasily in our seats
as a florid Catholic priest took the stage.
Obviously used to much smaller gatherings
he saw this as the big one
he'd psyched himself up
a chance to save a few heathen souls
or maybe just a chance to show off.
Anyway, he started talking.
For a long time.
Not about Veronica, of course – he'd never met her

Hers was just another coffin in a conveyor belt
another date in a diary
although he did of course say
that he'd met her family
a few days before
and that after a couple of hours
he felt he'd 'known them all his life…'
No, he talked about himself
his church
what he did all day
Then he tried to talk about Veronica
and got her name wrong, calling her Pat
Then he posthumously remarried her
to the aforementioned ex-spouse
Then he talked about 'her faith'
- the supposed faith of a humanist he'd never met -
and how 'sustaining' it must have been
which made me angry, and queasy
and I steeled myself for the next bit.
Oh yes, I knew the next platitude which was coming.
People had said the same thing to me
as a ten-year-old, when my father died,
but that didn't stem the surge of bile to my throat.

"Of course' he said, 'Veronica is now much happier
than we are…
she's gone to a better place'.

My nails dug into my palms.
I wanted to stand up and scream
'You charlatan! You fraud! You hypocrite!
This warm, lovely woman – mother, friend, lover –
is dead.
Cold.
Oblivious.
Gone forever.
In a few minutes her remains will be burned.
We'll never see her again.
She no longer exists.

Heart On My Sleeve

I'll tell you how dead she is –
if there was one spot of life left in her
she'd sit bolt upright in her coffin
and tell you to stop talking such a steaming pile
of false, patronising crap!
She's dead!
And she's in a better place than us?
We who are alive?
Breathing, conscious, thinking.
Perhaps happy, fulfilled, inspired, loving and creative.
Perhaps sad, lonely, underachieving and inadequate.
But aware!
Blood coursing, hearts beating, lungs pumping,
thoughts racing
and AWARE!
You don't really believe all that nonsense yourself,
do you?
Because if you did, you'd have thrown yourself
under a bus long ago
so that you could go to that 'better place' too…
You're just a confidence trickster!
If someone pointed a gun at your head
and cocked the trigger
you'd beg for your life, just like any of us would
you wouldn't say 'Go on, make my day, send me to
that better place….'
you'd piss yourself and beg to live –
you don't believe a word you're saying!'

But of course, I said nothing.
None of us said anything.
No-one ever says anything like that
on such an occasion
we just fidgeted, and remembered Veronica
in our own way
as the florid, winy-nosed, holy water splashing fool
pontificated on
and I vowed once more
as I urge you all

to squeeze every last drop of sweetness
from this thing we have called Life.
To take it in all its richness and celebrate it.
To do everything we can to improve its quality for
all of us who share this planet – now.
To celebrate Life
Because Life is what we are –
It's our one chance
all biological, empirical and, yes,
philosophical logic
tells us:
This is all there is.
Make it worthwhile.

Later, after the funeral,
in Veronica's sitting room
where six weeks before I'd given
a copy of my book
to our friend, shrunken and grey
with the terrible mark of liver cancer
and wondered what the hell to write inside
- I put 'love and total solidarity'
and left it at that –
I talked to her ex-husband.
I'd never met him before.
She'd divorced him gently some years previously
but they had remained friends
he obviously still cared deeply for her
and was terribly sad.
'Tomorrow' he said
'we'll go to the little plot I've bought
and put the ashes in it
and then that's it.'
And the simple words of that gentle man
in their terrible, loving finality
contrasted so totally with the rubbish
which had gone before.
I looked at him, smiled slightly,
said nothing.

Heart On My Sleeve

Of course, in all the ways which make us human
In the best sense
that isn't it.
Memories of Veronica will live long
in the hearts of those who love her
her sterling genes will be passed on
through her children
in the way of our biology, our identity, our species
but yes, dear friend, of course…

The door clanged shut.
We drove away from her home for the last time.
Joy looked back once and quietly said
'Goodbye, Veronica.'
That was all.

1995

TWO CANS OF ZYWIEC

Trevor was a farmer, co-owner of Coombes Farm with his sister Jenny. When Glastonwick, the beer and music festival I have co-organised for the past 25 years, was thrown out of its previous location a decade ago, Trevor and Jenny offered us a new home there. We had ten wonderful years partying together. I read this poem at his funeral.

In memory of Trevor Passmore

We came from two worlds and we met in the middle.
Dear Trev, I'm so sad that your time had to end.
A poem of thanks for the great years you gave us -
You started as landlord and finished as friend.

When I had that first interview with you and Jenny
I could see in your face you thought 'What have we here?
A bunch of pissed Lefties led by this loud nutter
Want space on our farm for their punk rock and beer!'

But soon we convinced you, and straight off, you loved it.
You got a new family, we got one too.
We found a beautiful home for our festival.
You found a home with the Glastonwick crew.

Then things got poignant. A shared diagnosis
Around the same time. We talked of our fears.
'Seems you're the lucky one, John.' Then you told me.
'Seems I am, Trev' I said, holding back tears.

Now we love real ale, but you always liked Zywiec.
The town and the people there, not just the beer.
When I came to see you on that final visit
As I cycled over, I got an idea.

I went to an offie, bought two cans of Zywiec.
I got there just ten minutes after you've gone.
They'll stand on your bar as a tribute this Glastonwick.
There in your memory. Life carries on.

2017

BOB CROW

There was a man who stood his ground.
Fought every inch, and won the day.
His legacy, his members' lot:
Good work conditions, decent pay.
By Tories and their tabloid dupes
And those who seek more than their share
Just like Millwall, his favourite team,
He wasn't liked, and didn't care.

But those who worked in transport knew
Their leader stood right by their side.
No management could lay them low:
They wore their union badge with pride.
He spoke for passengers as well:
Safety, not profit, always first.
Opposing fatal funding cuts -
Paddington, Potters Bar the worst.

Bob Crow. A boxer's grandson, he:
Led with the left and packed a punch.
The bosses knew he'd take them on:
No smarmy smile, no cosy lunch.
We need more like him, that's for sure:
Upfront and honest to the last.
He bargained hard and kept his word.
A union leader unsurpassed.

As zero hours contracts grow
And bosses offer Hobson's choice
Let us not mourn, but organize:
Get off our knees and find our voice!
This man worked hard for workers' rights:
A fair wage, a safe, steady job.
So join a union and stand firm.
That's the best way to honour Bob.

2014

RED WEDGWOOD

'The former Viscount Stansgate'
The Tory press would sneer.
'What does he know of struggle?
He's just a toffy peer!'
But it's not where you come from
It's what you bloody DO.
John Peel and Engels knew that
And Strummer knew it too.
A fighter for the working class:
A giant among men.
He wasn't Viscount Stansgate –
His name was Tony Benn.

2014

LITTLE MAN, BIG HEART

Dedicated to the memory of Adrian More, and to the Poulter family who did so much to help him.

It's only a record, I said to myself:
and indeed it was
only a record.
Anarchy in the UK
on EMI
in the black sleeve.
One of two copies I'd queued up to buy
on the day it came out
in 1976
from the indie record store
in Canterbury High Street -
the other given to my then girlfriend
at Kent University
who was into Boston.
I had more than a feeling
she didn't like it
because she threw it in the bin.
(She wasn't my girlfriend for long,
but not because of that.)
I showed it to you one day
and you said
'Wow! That's really rare!
I'm going to this punk disco on Saturday!
Can I borrow it?'
I knew I'd never see it again
and I didn't care.

So much of who we are
is where and who we come from.
You weren't born with a silver spoon.
You didn't even get Daltrey's plastic one.
You grew up in Barnardo's.
Your home not so much broken
as atomized

before it had even existed.
A book of regulations for a mum and dad,
hand-me-down clothes,
hand-me-down life.
But you had spirit.
Some lovely people befriended you
and although nobody
could ever really cure that ache
where your family should have been
they gave you hope
and the strength to try.
When I met you
you were really trying.
Really, really trying.

And yes, you could be really trying!
For those who didn't know
about the hole
in the centre of your life
your antics
in that constant search for human acceptance
for friendship
- for love -
could seem over-the-top, desperate.
But I think I understood.
I took you with me to a gig:
the local punks couldn't fathom out
the little, shouty, needy, hyperactive bloke
who looked like a greaser
and wanted to hang out with them
and some offered only rejection -
after what you had been through
the hardest thing of all.
That's why I gave you that Sex Pistols single.
I hoped.
I imagined you swaggering into the disco
waving it
in your brave, false-confident way.
'Bloody hell mate! Where did you get that?'

Heart On My Sleeve

I imagined the inevitable story you'd make up.
I knew I'd never see that record again:
I knew it would get nicked,
or scratched, or broken, or covered in beer, or lost
but I hoped it would give you a tiny foothold
in the latest of the many little worlds
you were trying to be a part of.
And to be honest
I never liked the Pistols much anyway
and I wish they had called the bloody thing
'Disciplined, Clear-Minded Socialist Organisation In The UK
(With Clean Underpants)'
because it would have saved me loads of time-consuming, irritating arguments
down the years -
but that's another matter entirely.

I don't know what happened
to you, or the single, that night
but I do know that my mate Steve tried to help:
I know that you liked and trusted me.
When I went to Belgium
in 1979
to play music and organise
you followed me
- despite all your problems
resourcefulness was your middle name -
and we put you back on the train to England
just before the riot.
Although you'd have absolutely loved it
a riot was the last thing you needed:
your whole life had been one -
and not in the way Billy Bragg meant.
There were some more stories
some more scrapes
and then poetry, music and the world took over.
I lost touch with you
and the people who were helping you
but I never forgot you, or them

and when I heard 'Anarchy in the UK'
I'd often think of that single in the black sleeve
of your cheeky smile
the leather jacket
the friendly elbow in the ribs
and I'd wonder how brave little Sisyphus from Essex
was coping with the boulder
that life had made
his constant companion.

Then a couple of years ago
after yet another punk rock funeral
I caught up with your long-time friend and protectress.
She told me that you were very ill:
that your life had been more of the same really -
the smiles, the scrapes,
the resourcefulness against all odds,
the determination to make the best of things,
that old boulder going up and down the hill.
I'm sorry I never got to see you again.

Farewell, mate.
The boulder is still now.
But when it rolled down to the bottom
you never stopped trying
to push it back up again –
more often than not
with a great big smile on your face.
Little man.
Big heart.

2016

M.C. ATTILA

CORO NATION
A late addition, March 2020. For obvious reasons...

This little rap's here to inspire us
Not to get Coronavirus
Lady Gaga, Miley Cyrus
They don't want Coronavirus
It's a disease carried on the breeze
And none of us would like it please
It's a disease carried on the breeze
(Piss off Trump, it's not 'Chinese!')

Bloody hell! It's a pandemic
Running through the world at a rate systemic
(Just to spell out my position
I'm 62 with a lung condition)
Let's all try hard to avoid it
Till researchers have destroyed it
Don't get cranky, don't be a fogey -
Use that hanky, bin that bogey!

This little rap's here to inspire us
Not to get Coronavirus
Lady Gaga, Miley Cyrus
They don't want Coronavirus
It's a disease carried on the breeze
And none of us would like it please
It's a disease carried on the breeze
(Piss off Trump, it's not 'Chinese!')

Please be kind and give assistance
In a way that keeps a distance
Get your normal shopping done -
There's enough for everyone
Panic buying? Stupid caper.
Put back all that toilet paper.
What a crappy, shit idea.
Local pub delivers BEER!

This little rap's here to inspire us
Not to get Coronavirus
Lady Gaga, Miley Cyrus
They don't want Coronavirus
It's a disease carried on the breeze
And none of us would like it please
It's a disease carried on the breeze
(Piss off Trump, it's not 'Chinese!')

New dance called the Pontius Pilate.
Time we all learn to freestyle it
Water, hands and a bar of soap -
Clean under a microscope
(No, don't scratch your dirty bridge
Then go down and raid the fridge)
Please keep safe and please keep well.
CORONOVIRUS – GO TO HELL…

FORTY YEARS IN RHYME

This piece charts the development of spoken word. Not even a genre when I started 40 years ago, it is now a massive part of the live performance scene – in all its forms. Rap is a part of it, I've always had an affinity with the rhythm and over the years have written quite a few. They just fit in alongside everything else in my live shows. Here is a selection.

Forty years in rhyme
Thirty-eight full time
I'm still in my prime
Life has been sublime
I could use some music
Someone else can choose it
If it helps me flow
And you've got it won't refuse it
Maybe not the done thing
Maybe it's a young thing
I don't chat no gun thing
No mad Kim Jong Un thing
I'm here to enlighten
Representing Brighton
Now we're in the Premier League
Who we gonna frighten?
My ends are southernmost
I'm from the Sussex coast
Hoes are in the garden centre
Bread is simply toast
Don't give me no cup of tea
When I'm getting uppity
Beer is my cup of tea
High specific gravity
Like a wind I'm blowing
Like a river flowing
Forty years of knowing
Exactly where I'm going
Sixty on the planet
Spoken word I span it
Ranting verse I ran it
Seagull not a gannet
Checking out fresh styles

Bringing tears and smiles
From the Outer Hebrides
To the Seven Dials
Old punk on a new trip
Not a tried and true trip
Not a 'dissing you' trip
Not a sniffing glue trip
Beer I like it hoppy
Verse I like it stroppy
Sometimes I get personal
But I don't like it soppy.

I remember Brother D
Grandmaster was legendary
But U-Roy was the first to show
Toasters started off this flow
Ranting verse, reggae chat
Hip hop, grime and all of that
We are simply spoken word
Voices shouting to be heard
Respect to my fellow man
From Cooper Clarke to Yellowman
Stormzy, Tempest and Luke Wright.
Spoken word is doing alright.
When I began there was no scene
Looking back at all that's been
40 years of spitting rhyme
Having a fantastic time!

2019

SUBSTITUTE

Being a performance poet I am versatile, travel easily and am able to do emergency gigs at very short notice. This poem was inspired by a few of the most memorable occasions when I've come off the bench, as it were. Dedicated to the utterly brilliant Sleaford Mods, to the great poets Linton Kwesi Johnson and John Cooper Clarke, and, yes, to Donny Osmond. It was an honour, chaps. (Football reference: CMS was one of the most hard-working and likeable players ever to wear a Brighton shirt, and was one of our star players when I wrote this.)

Saturday evening, Evening Star
Had a lot of beer, didn't have to walk far
Round to the Albert to see Sleaford Mods
Two really sharp, really sussed, really shouty sods
Up to the bar for another pint of beer
Pissed off promoter. 'Jason's not here.
Crashed out in London on a settee'.
Crowd came for Jason – they got me!

Filled in for Linton, filled in for Clarkie
Filled in at Glasto while they hunted for a sparkie
Filled in for Donny Osmond and that's not a myth
But I'll never be a sub for Craig Mackail-Smith
No I'll never be a sub for Craig Mackail-Smith

Swindon Town Hall didn't go to plan -
I was the support act, waiting for the man
Just like the Velvets, waiting for the man
Waiting waiting waiting waiting waiting for the man.
Man didn't show, to everyone's regret
Promoter says 'Wanna do another set?'
Crowd came for Linton, got two sets from me
All's well that ends well - I got his fee!

Filled in for Linton, filled in for Clarkie
Filled in at Glasto while they hunted for a sparkie
Filled in for Donny Osmond and that's not a myth
But I'll never be a sub for Craig Mackail-Smith
No I'll never be a sub for Craig Mackail-Smith

These days it gives me enormous pleasure
That the great Johnny Clarke is a national treasure
But there was a time when things were iffy
He could turn up, let's say, a bit squiffy!
One night he never even turned up at all
Hapless promoter gave me a call
'He's not here, Attila, do you want to do a set?'
Jumped in a cab with a quick 'You bet!'

Filled in for Linton, filled in for Clarkie
Filled in at Glasto while they hunted for a sparkie
Filled in for Donny Osmond and that's not a myth
But I'll never be a sub for Craig Mackail-Smith
No I'll never be a sub for Craig Mackail-Smith

Late 1980s Glastonbury -
Disaster in the Cabaret Marquee.
PA out of action, generator broke.
'I'll do a set, I'm a really shouty bloke!'
Thousand people, great big tent -
Meant what I said and I said what I meant.
Standing ovation for giving it a go
Generator mended, on with the show!

Filled in for Linton, filled in for Clarkie
Filled in at Glasto while they hunted for a sparkie
Filled in for Donny Osmond and that's not a myth
But I'll never be a sub for Craig Mackail-Smith
No I'll never be a sub for Craig Mackail-Smith

Donny Osmond was booked to play the Marquee
Too scared to fly so they asked me.
One day's notice. 'Come on Attila -
Fill in for Donny, it'll be a real thriller...'
Now it's never been in my plans
To do a gig for Donny Osmond fans
Though half were quickly out the door
The rest really liked it – I got an encore!

Heart On My Sleeve

Filled in for Linton, filled in for Clarkie
Filled in at Glasto while they hunted for a sparkie
Filled in for Donny Osmond and that's not a myth
But I'll never be a sub for Craig Mackail-Smith
No I'll never be a sub for Craig Mackail-Smith

I'm shit at football and not just a bit -
Really really really really really really really shit.
Worse than a donkey, can't control the ball
Can't head, can't shoot, can't pass, bugger all.
All my life I've thought it's a shame
I'm useless at my favourite game -
Try as I might I've two left feet.
Too old now so my fate's complete.

Filled in for Linton, filled in for Clarkie
Filled in at Glasto while they hunted for a sparkie
Filled in for Donny Osmond and that's not a myth
But I'll never be a sub for Craig Mackail-Smith
No I'll never be a sub for Craig Mackail-Smith

I can tell you now without getting stressy -
If I filled in for CMS things would turn...

Messi.

2014

TALKING 'BOUT MY GENERATION (Who?)
A reggae talkover piece, inspired by Roger Daltrey's 'thoughts' on Brexit.

I'm ashamed of my generation
It's not a generalisation
There are loads I see think just like me
But I'm seething with frustration
I'm ashamed of my generation
Once crusty now crustacean
Then mod or punk now spouting junk
In our strange divided nation
For years the right wing press been spammin'
Down our throats their bigotry rammin'
Murdoch and Dacre been programmin'
Brains full of hateful nonsense crammin'
No desire to cross examine
State of intellectual famine
You call me snowflake I call you gammon
(Hang on a minute I think I'm a gammon...
Though if I'm pink I'd rather be a salmon...
But if I'm a gammon I'm a left wing gammon...
DIY – no love for mammon...)
 I'm ashamed of my generation
Obsessed with immigration
Loads of young folk think we're a joke
With the brains of a dead alsatian
I'm ashamed of my generation
They're such a strange mutation
From the Summer of Love to 'Heavens above -
Give the Tories a donation!'
Horizons shrinking as they get older
Hearts and minds growing harder and colder
Hippy garlands left to moulder
Poor and sick get the cold shoulder
Slowly losing their love for humanity
I'm alright jack selfish inanity
Some in church claim Christianity
Jesus Christ would call it insanity

Heart On My Sleeve

But we know we're not all like that
Call your mates out when they spout tat
And your in-laws when they spout tat
And your sister when she spouts tat
And your brother when he spouts tat
Sixty doesn't mean right wing prat
Seventy doesn't mean sad old bat
Eighty bring out the welcome mat
Ninety wear a big hippie hat
I'm reclaiming our generation
With great determination
For unity, community,
Warm hearts and INTEGRATION!

2019

CRIME WRITER

Who's the killer, the bigger killer?
Who is ill and who is iller?
Who's the killer, the bigger killer?
Here's a tale from MC Attila

White estate, some newtown overspill
Kind of place where life's always uphill
They know the score, same shit, same dice to roll
Football, boxing, music or the dole
Some rise up and shine, some burn and die
Most look out for the best way to get by
One just can't find any way at all
Blank eyes stare at a dead end brick wall

Who's the killer, the bigger killer?
Who is ill and who is iller?
Who's the killer, the bigger killer?
Here's a tale from MC Attila

Back from a two hour full-on liquid lunch
London journo lines up another punch
People he's not met, places he's never been
Soft targets for his hack spleen
Immigrants of course, at number one
Endless stories, endless source of fun
Two men, two worlds, both men dead inside…
One more man then we'll watch three worlds collide….

Who's the killer, the bigger killer?
Who is ill and who is iller?
Who's the killer, the bigger killer?
Hear this tale from MC Attila

Third man comes from somewhere far away
Thought with prayers and love he'd be OK
Prayers and love stopped when the wars began
Fled with his family, as would any man
Two long years they had to run and roam

Heart On My Sleeve

Wept with joy when they got their new home
Run down flat in newtown white estate
Near someone with too much time to hate...

Who's the killer, the bigger killer?
Who is ill and who is iller?
Who's the killer, the bigger killer?
Hear this tale from MC Attila

Hack's in the pub as the presses start to roll
Headline screams 'Asylum on the dole!'
Yes, more tired and cliche ridden crap
Just enough to make a strung out string snap
Blank eyes stares at the tabloid's front page
Kicks the wall in dumb, frustrated rage
Heads for home and grabs a petrol can
Then goes hunting for his fellow man...

Who's the killer, the bigger killer?
Who is ill and who is iller?
Who's the killer, the bigger killer?
That's the question from MC Attila

Awful screams as the murder flames bite
Horror strikes and death lights up the night
Blank eyes picked up the very next day
Hack's there at his desk, tapping away
'Lock him up and throw away the key!'
Wallows in his foul hypocrisy
Who's most to blame for this evil deed?
He who acts or he who sows the seed?

Who's the killer, the bigger killer?
Who is ill and who is iller?
Who's the killer, the bigger killer?
Make your choice...

says MC Attila

2006

THE IRON MEN OF RAP!

I was very sad when the fad for gangsta rap came in around 1989, and even sadder when it took everything over like a big, bloated monster and consigned the conscious rappers to the sidelines. Written to the riff of 'Iron Man' by Black Sabbath.

You're the iron men rappers with your big gold chains
You talk like the clappers but you don't use your brains
The Grandmaster's Message made me hold my breath
But now I'd rather listen to Lawnmower Deth!
You rap about your gold and you rap about your car
And you rap about what good rappers you are
You rap about your guns and the money you make
And the size of your one eyed trouser snake
You say it's bigger than the Albert Hall
But I bet it's like an earthworm, very very small
You say it's bigger than the Albert Hall
But I bet it's like a maggot or you ain't got one at all!
You run on stage with your guns in a rage
Like angry prisoners fresh out of the cage
Your finger's on the trigger and you want to engage
Turning on the chill in the new Ice Age
And there's violence, violence in the air
But some of you want it, you don't seem to care
And there's violence, violence in the air
But some of you want it, you don't seem to care
Now I don't like the dollar and I don't like the gun
And the (w)rapping they come in don't bother me none
I wanna rap fast and I wanna have fun
And I mean have fun not shoot someone!

With your massive testicles and concrete cock
Gonna bust a gonad every time you rock
Every move in your body is designed to shock
So yo! there, preacher, how's your flock?
Now I don't wanna hear about segregation
Don't wanna hear about your perfect nation
Don't wanna hear about Farrakhan
Cos Farrakhan is an evil man
And hey, everybody, let's make a show

Heart On My Sleeve

'Cos if Farrakhan gets you you're gonna blow
From the hair on my head to my hairy scro'
I'm out of the bottle and I'm ready to blow!

The rap I rap is black and white
This rap says unionise, don't fight
This rap doesn't wallow in liberal guilt
It just says equal up to the hilt
This rap's got a penis of average size
Not a huge great whale flopping out of its flies
No gold, no chains, no hype, no lies
Just a thinking brain and a pair of sharp eyes
So wise up rappers and before you spout
Find something original to rap about!
I've had my say now it's over and out
From MC Attila – the poetry tout
Said MC Attila – signing out!

1989

BOYS IN THE HOOD (Trainspotter Rap)

But, of course, not all rappers conform to this crude stereotype. MC Trainspotter, the world's first ever rapping trainspotter, certainly doesn't. He knows that you don't have to live somewhere really tough and have a gun and a big penis to be a rapper...

MC Trainspotter, yeah, that's me
And this is my homeboy, Nice-T!
Now some people think that trainspotting's rot
But me and my posse we say 'It's not!'
All you need is a camera, notebook and pen
You write down a number then you write one down again
We're ignored by the nation, we go down the station
And we've got another hobby –
Masturbation
Hey don't walk away, cos I'm talking to you
You know what they call us –
The Platform Two Live Crew!
Now me and my homeboys work in a bank
And at the weekend, we go to the library
On Saturday mornings we like shopping
and then we go amateur league groundhopping
I nearly caught pneumonia at Billingham Synthonia
Wanna know the layout of the ground?
I'll phone ya
I was filled with euphoria at Northwich Victoria
Wanna know the layout of the ground?
I'll bore ya
And at half time I've got everything I need
A nice telephone directory to read
Yes, MC Trainspotter in the house
I've got the suss and I've got the nous
I don't live in a ghetto like those rappers in the States
I like the police, yes, they're my best mates
I've never been arrested, that goes without saying
I've reported everybody I've seen travelling without paying
And here's what I say to every other rapping crew –
I'm OK at rapping but I'm not as good as you
But I do think you spend far too much on your gear
I could save you some money so please listen here

Heart On My Sleeve

My trainers come from Oxfam and they cost 50p
My anorak's my mum's and the carrier bag was free
I wouldn't wear a gold chain, somebody might mug me
And I don't want a baseball cap, they really bug me
We're the parka posse – we're the boys in the hood
And it keeps out the rain – now isn't that good?
And if you want information down at the station
Just ask me, it'll fill me with elation
MC Trainspotter, yeah, that's me
Yo! there homeboy!
Want a cup of tea?

1991

RADIO RAP!

The state of Radio One in 1983. My first rap 12 inch.

I turned on the radio this afternoon
with half a brain for a mindless tune
and if you want some mindless fun
it's always there on Radio One
The braincell level is very low
a diminished braincell ratio
and if your IQ's under five
it's just the stuff to keep you alive.
Synth pop and electrofunk
and endless hours of boring junk –
if that reflects our nation's taste
then this generation's gone to waste!
So where's the challenge? Where's the news?
Where's the ones who'll light the fuse?
Well I can see them all around
but they never make the DJ sound
'cos the senile programmers get the bird
if they hear an idea or a naughty word
so all we get to pass the days
are endless boring pop clichés
LIKE
shake your booty on the floor
hang your wombat out the door
whomp that flounder, hit that plaice
wrap that turbot round my face
save your love cos the girl is mine
get on down, it's disco time
OK yar and I'm alright
The happy sound on a Saturday night!
And then on top of that powerful stuff
If you didn't think that was rough enough
The daytime DJs cap the lot –
They should be rounded up and shot!
If you want to hear a real prize prune
try Steve Wright In The Afternoon
the biggest fruit bat of them all

Heart On My Sleeve

he'll REALLY drive you up the wall!
Like a plughole clogged with pubic hair
Young Mister Wright clogs up the air
and everyone can surely see
that he needs a lobotomy!
There's one man got the feel, it's true –
good old John Peel he talks to you –
but most of the rest are as bland as could be
with the taste of a tench and the flair of a flea
so stuff it, stuff it Radio One
the happy sound that's really dumb
Bring back the pirates, they had class
And STICK YOUR PROGRAMMES UP YOUR ARSE!

NEW WORLD ORDER RAP
'We will not let the mechanisms of death fall into the hands of men with no respect for life'
(George Bush, 12/3/02)

Change the names and fudge the dates
For United Nations read United States
They're coming soon over your border
One World Nightmare - New World Order....

Yes, they talk of Jesus Christ: Self Righteous Brothers all
And every television screen is at their beck and call
So here's a public service broadcast: he who lives, obeys
and the moral of this story is just what the dollar says..

There's no debate, there's just G8 and a global mafia superstate
Policed by thugs, awash with drugs and kept in place by Murdoch's mugs
And Sheriff USA is there to turn you into fries
Yes you can bank on a Yank in a tank 'cos he who argues, dies!

Change the names and fudge the dates
For United Nations read United States
They're coming soon over your border
One World Nightmare - New World Order ....

If you try to play the game you're sure to get it wrong
'cos the New World Order makes the rules up as it goes along
One minute you're its bosom pal and general factotum
The next its high technology is aimed straight at your ....head

Said sell you arms, said bomb you flat.
Said sell you arms, said bomb you flat.
Said sell you arms, then bomb you flat.
Then sell you more arms...fancy that!

You want to join another gang? Hey look, your country just went bang!

Change the names and fudge the dates
For United Nations read United States
Fundamentalists were their friends
Are they still? Well, that depends....

Heart On My Sleeve

Al Quaeda - now they'll bleed ya!
You'll end up just like roast pork.
They paid you to murder kids
in Commie countries, not New York!

Hey Assad, you made 'em mad
Lockerbie bomb was really bad
But now they want you on their side
So they'll forget the ones who died

Hey Saddam, time for bam-bam
They backed you against Iran
But Saudi oil is looking.....dodgy.
So they're gonna waste ya, podgy!

Change the names and fudge the dates
For United Nations read United States.....
They're coming soon over the border
One World Nightmare - New World Order...

Hail Humanitarian Nato - thats not a bomb, it's a potato!
Just behave or dig your grave: they've got some refugees to save
It's pick and choose, some win, some lose - yes, they're in Kosovo
But Palestine, Timor, Rwanda, sorry, man, no go
Hey, it's not that they don't care, but there aren't points to score down there
The message is to Moscow, large - shut up and put up, they're in charge
And they don't want to lose contacts for banking loans and arms contracts
For every psychopath they bomb there are two more they buy stuff from
And sell stuff to and arm and train and arm again and arm again

Said arm again said Armageddon
Said arm again said Armageddon
Said evil thug – said trusted friend
said evil thug – said trusted friend....

Change the names and fudge the dates
For United Nations read United States
for NATO read the Pentagon
They rule the world: the reds are gone

Attila The Stockbroker

Now Mary had a little lamb: its fleece was white as snow
But when the CIA found out that lamb was sure to go
There WAS a Grand Old Duke of York, he HAD ten thousand men
But the New World Order carpet bombed them till he had just ten
And then they signed a big arms deal - now he's got lots again...
The Serbs the Serbs have funny verbs and don't use vowels in their words!

Change the names and fudge the dates
For United Nations read United States
Said G8, IMF, World Bank.
Put a fascist in your tank.
Get a loan, then starve the poor -
Then they'll let you have some more.
That's the way the world is run.
Gorbachev - what have you done?

1995

TELL SID HE'D BETTER BUY HIS MUM A JUMPER

Anyone old enough will surely remember the 'Tell Sid' British Gas share advertising campaign in 1986 which started off the whole Thatcherite privatization nightmare. Well, Sid's much older now and the chickens have come home to roost. This was my first ever reggae talkover poem, recorded over a track from the brilliant Rebel Control.

Tell Sid he'd better buy his mum a jumper
Tell Sid he'd better buy her one or two
Cos she's getting very old and it's getting very cold
And she doesn't know just what she's gonna do
Tell Sid he'd better buy his mum a jumper
Tell Sid he'd better buy her one today
'Cos her gas bill's come and her feet are going numb
And she doesn't know just how she's gonna pay

Tell Sid he'd better buy his mum a jumper
Tell Sid he'd better buy her three or four
'Cos all she wants to do is cry, all she wants to do is die
When she hears the bailiffs banging on the door
Tell Sid he'd better buy his mum a jumper
Tell Sid he'd better hang his head in shame
A mother and a wife who worked hard all her life
Now she's cold and alone and Sid's to blame

CHORUS
For regeneration
Of this greed ravaged nation
We need renationalisation
Without compensation
For regeneration
Of this greed ravaged nation
We need renationalisation
Without compensation

Tell Sid he'd better buy his mum a jumper
Tell Sid he'd better buy her five or six
Cos he should have used his brain, not been conned yet again
By the Tories and their privatizing tricks

Tell Sid he'd better buy his mum a jumper
Cos it's she who pays the price for what he did
When he joined the sorry mass who bought shares in British Gas
Sold our heritage to make themselves a quid

Tell Sid he'd better buy his mum a jumper
Tell Sid he'd better buy her seven or eight
He's a scared little mouse in his cosy little house
As he sees the anger turning into hate
Tell Sid he'd better buy his mum a jumper
Tell Sid he should have thought of that before
'Cos when the poor find their voice there will be a stark choice
Civil society - or civil war

CHORUS
For regeneration
Of this greed ravaged nation
We need renationalisation
Without compensation
For regeneration
Of this greed ravaged nation
We need renationalisation
Without compensation

And if the bankers' press wail
Occupy the Daily Mail
And shut down the Sun –
Let justice be done

Tell Sid he'd better buy his mum a jumper
Tell Sid he'd better buy her nine or ten
But he did what he was told when Royal Mail was sold
And he went and bought a load of shares again
Tell Sid he'd better buy his mum a jumper
Cos it really is about time that he did

But he's 'So Busy, Dear'.
Visits three times a year.

So if she dies cold and alone -
Tell Sid.

2013

COMIC IN A BASKET

A rap about why I haven't done a comedy gig since 1991.

This is the tale of my times, the place where I started from
The friends and contemporaries I've now parted from
A story of belief and pride, of how it has to be
For Attila MC
It's all about perspective, compromise, choices
Paths going different ways, different voices
Those who gave up and those who still attack
And want to talk back
It's all about England in these dull old days
Where everyone obeys
And hacks say it's 'old hat' to shout the odds and seethe
And say what you believe
It's the battle of ideas and the fight for proper beers
And it's going to go on for years and years and years
I stand for my words and for decent beer too
If you advertise chemical piss, this rap's for you -
I'd rather sniff glue.

Talking cutting edge gone blunt, blunt, blunt
Talking saboteurs now riding with the hunt
Talking cutting edge gone blunt, blunt, blunt
Talking saboteurs now riding with the hunt
Right in your face and I'm not gonna mask it -
MC Attila on the case
Of the comic in a basket.

I've earned my living as a poet since 1982
Didn't know it was that long? Well, now you do.
In fact I started out a couple of years before
Blagged spots at punk gigs: they wanted more!
Peel sessions, album, gigs in the rock scene
Going to places most poets had never been
But then a whole new scene began
It was a good plan
Sure, from time to time it could get a bit tame
But it was a fine game

London circuit – they called it New Variety
Some kind of underground cultural society
A new breed got the chance to spread the word
And get our voices heard.
For three or four years we all stood together
- Poets, musicians, comedians, whatever -
As long as you were sharp and had something to say
The people were with you: it was OK…..
Then defeat on defeat on defeat on defeat
Put the whole of our culture on the retreat
And a radical attack was no longer hip.
All the rats left the sinking ship.

New Variety became 'alternative comedy'
Losing all its cultural diversity.
Alternative comedy became 'new comedy'
Losing its political suss and energy.
New comedy became simply 'comedy'
Corporate mainstream TV commodity.
'Got a new ad for Aims of Industry?
I'm a comedian – give it to me!'
Now comedy's so dull and safe and bland
It's time to make a stand
No bite, no attitude, it's not even funny -
And it's all about money.
Gag every ten seconds or you're history
Scriptwriting gag team; comedy factory.
Roll on, roll off:
Are you with the agency?
'Too controversial; no good for TV!'
Comedy to go. Careers in comedy.
Comic in a basket.
Comedy package. Corporate hospitality.
Comic in a basket.
Seventies TV, adverts, shopping:
Routine routine.
Seventies TV, old people, shopping:
Routine routine.
'Very funny' (Daily Express)

Heart On My Sleeve

Comic in a basket.
'Hilarious' (Daily Mail)
Comic in a basket.
Get your dicks out for the banks
And give your sponsors grateful thanks.
Perrier? Piss. Perrier? Piss. Perrier? Piss.
I ain't new to this…
Edinburgh Fringe?
Comedy trade fair.
Miss it if you dare.
Movers and shakers.
Radio and TV.
Me! Me! Me! Me!

Talking cutting edge gone blunt, blunt, blunt
Talking saboteurs now riding with the hunt
Talking cutting edge gone blunt, blunt, blunt
Talking saboteurs now riding with the hunt…..

Punter in a basket comedy club –
Braying student Sun reader fun pub
'Tell us a joke or we'll get rough
And lay off that political poetry stuff!'
But politics is people's lives, not fashion
And I burn with passion
My culture and beliefs run very deep
And I'm no sheep
So one fine day I handed in my cards
Didn't find it hard…..
Bollocks to comedy – I've got my own scene
Rock 'n' roll poet, Sydney to Aberdeen
Life is humour, music, politics, rage:
I want them all on stage!
But I keep in touch with my old friends
And I'm hip to the trends
I watch the scene from time to time and curse:
It's getting worse…

The Browbeaten Broadcasting Corporation
Cowed by years of intimidation
Is putting out pap that's reached a brand new low:
Bass – how low can you go?
Throwaway garbage game show lobotomese.
Mad Cower Disease!
'Wanna be the star of 'Tacky Tabloid Tease?'
'Ooh ooh yes please!'
Comic in a basket's radio TV game show
About game shows in history.
'What's that advert from '73?
Who was in that situation comedy?'
Crap TV about crap TV.
Radio in need of radiotherapy.
Recycled sheep in a bovine society.
Audiovisual BSE.

Gland in hand in the land of the bland: no stand
- Comic in a basket.
'Keep to the script as planned or you'll get banned!'
- Comic in a basket.
Some of you were mates, I don't want to offend ya
But I'm rapping for a brand new agenda…..
Talking cutting edge gone blunt, blunt, blunt
Talking saboteurs now riding with the hunt
Talking cutting edge gone blunt, blunt, blunt
Talking saboteurs now riding with the HUNT!

1993

SPIRIT OF THE AGE
(2006, rewritten 2020)

You've got to be young and black to rap, right?
So I've no chance 'cos I'm old, punk rock and white...
You've got to be young and black to rap? Wrong!
Anyone can rap - or write a punk rock song
So don't look at me with scorn or derision
I don't accept boundaries of cultural division
I'm MC Attila and I'm right in your face
So listen up folks 'cos I ain't going no place
This rap's called 'Spirit Of The Age'
All my life I'm gonna be on stage
Millions of ideas buzzing round my head
I'll be rapping till the day I'm dead
Aged 48 I wasn't sedate
Rancid rule, Joe Strummer is my soul mate
49, I was doing just fine
Reeling in the Right on my verbal fishing line
Fifty? I was nifty!
So don't look at me like I'm sad or I'm shifty...
51, I'd have had some fun
If Brighton scored 10 and Crystal Palace scored none
52, I was talking to you -
And I made more sense than Blink 182...
53? Top of the tree!
Red rebel rhymes and rapping rebel poetry
54, like I said before -
Show me a fascist, I'll show him the floor
55 still cutting it live
While boring arty poets took a nose dive
56, I was high in the mix
This old punk rocker had learned some new tricks
57, still first eleven
Drinking real ale like it's manna from heaven

58, I was fuelling debate
Giving it straight from the 51st State
59, laying down the line
Pulling out words and watching them intertwine
60? Still demanding attention!
I wasn't drawing my punk rock pension...
As long as I'm alive I'll be live on stage:
Age of the spirit - spirit of the age!

JUST PLAIN REVOLTING

JOSEPH PORTER'S SLEEPING BAG

I thought perhaps it was a Slug
Maybe a Decomposing Rug
Or some Huge Condom, clogged with Clag –
It's Joseph Porter's Sleeping Bag...

A Mad Bacteriologist's Dream
Where Bell End Boursin reigns supreme
And even Bedbugs puke and gag –
It's Joseph Porter's Sleeping Bag...

The Outside festers and within
The Inside's grey as Major's Skin
A Quilted Dustbin, or a Rag -
It's Joseph Porter's Sleeping Bag...

No Launderette has crossed its Path
Folk Vomit in its Aftermath
There's Notebooks and a Railway Mag
In Joseph Porter's Sleeping Bag...

A Camel's Foreskin, by compare,
Smells sweeter than the Alpine Air!
I tell you this. I'd never shag
In Joseph Porter's Sleeping Bag...

THE FINAL ABLUTION

Stung by these words so rudely bawled
To Protag's old machine it crawled
A Scene too gruesome to be screened
The Day the Sleeping Bag was cleaned...

Industrial Agent was fetched.
The Traumatised Appliance retched.
Inside, a Sewer slowly sloshed
The day the Sleeping Bag was washed...

A Tidal Wave of Helmet Brie
Flowed, festering, towards the Sea
And in it Plague Rats gaily preened
The day the Sleeping Bag was cleaned...

The Foetid Futon's Foreskin Feta
Caused many an angry Greenpeace Letter!
'First Exxon Valdiz, now This!'
The Day the Hotpoint took the Piss...

And now the Horrid Thing is clean
And Lilac-Smelling and Pristine
There's still no way I'd ever shag
In Joseph Porter's Sleeping Bag!

THE NUPTUAL FIREPLACE

The Tale I now impart to you
(Improbable, perhaps, but True)
Concerns a Dame who asked one day
To breath the Quaggish Quilt's Bouquet...

She did not flinch as Bag came near
But sniffed without a Hint of Fear..
Somehow the Suppurating Sack
Became an Aphrodisiac!

Unfathomable Chemistry –
A Miracle of Alchemy!
Repository of Sweaty Scrotum
Now turned into a Lovers' Totem!

Bestow upon the Happy Pair
A Garland of Gonad Gruyere…
For now they sleep, all safe and snug
Beneath this Rank Rim Roquefort Rug

United! Hail the glorious Bag!
Beatify its sacred Clag!
And hang it, stuffed, in Oaken Case
Above the Nuptual Fireplace...

All 1994

THE RETURN OF WINTER VOMITING BUG

In the Seventies and Eighties there were loads of punk bands named after bodily functions and/or horrible diseases. The one in the title never actually existed, but all the others did - in one case, I believe, still do. This poem is dedicated to all those who remember the legendary gigs at the now-demolished George Robey pub in North London - high tide in the gents' toilets, dogshit on the stage. And no, there never was a pub called the Broken Toilet, although there were quite a few where a name change would have been appropriate back in the day – especially after a Crass gig.

I thought that they had gone for good.
A bloody tragic loss.
But then I got a flyer
at a Pukes gig in New Cross…
A solid wall of armpit stench
encased in rotting leather.
The kings of crust-anarcho-thrash
Are getting back together!

The flyer's here. Wow, what a line-up.
Take a look at this….
There's Dogshit Sandwich playing first,
The Bugs, then Seats of Piss!
Sick On The Bus are headlining.
You coming with me, mate?
The gig's at the George Robey. So?
It's been knocked down? That's great!

What's that? It's all a wind-up?
There isn't such a band?
Your memory's not what it was.
Of course I understand.
We saw them! Broken Toilet, Slough.
Way back in '81.
With Rudimentary Peni.
A classic gig, my son!

It's there we heard the Bugs first play
Their great anarcho song.
Yes. 'Smash the Cistern'. Fucking ACE.
Of course they spelt it wrong!
It was a pun. Real clever stuff.
The Broken Toilet, see...
They named the song after the pub.
Don't look like that at me!

They've got some brilliant T shirts too.
It's NOT a joke, you prat.
A big stag beetle, being sick,
Wearing a Santa hat!
One last time at the Robey, mate.
It's gonna be sublime...
It's not until April the First
So we've got loads of time!

2017

FOOTBALL

I have written poems about football all my life, and for nearly twenty years chronicled in verse the long battle to save Brighton & Hove Albion FC – a battle in which, as co-founder of our Independent Supporters' Association, I am proud to have played a part. These first two poems tell the story and the first one hangs on the wall in Dick's Bar, our supporters' bar at the stadium we campaigned so hard for. For many years, as well as being stadium announcer and match day DJ, I was Poet in Residence at Brighton & Hove Albion.

GOLDSTONE GHOSTS

As bulldozers close in upon our old, beloved home
and those who stand to profit rub their hands
so we gather here together in sad, angry disbelief
and for one last time our voices fill the stands.
This is no happy parting, but a battle-scarred farewell
though victory hopes are mingled with the tears
And I, like you, will stand here as the final whistle blows
with memories which echo down the years.....

The Chelsea fans threw pennies. Old ones. Sharpened. I was eight.
A target in the South Stand with my dad
And he got rather battered as he held me close and tight
and confirmed my view that Chelsea fans were mad!
And there, on those old wooden seats, I learned to love the game.
The sights and sounds exploded in my head.
My dad was proud to have a son with football in his blood -
but two short years later, he was dead.

Eleven. I went on my own. (My friends liked chess and stuff.)
'Now don't go in the North Stand!' said my mum.
But soon I did. Kit Napier's corner curled into the net.
Oh god. The Bournemouth Boot Boys! Better run....
Then Villa in the big crunch game. A thirty thousand crowd.
Bald Lochhead scored, but we still won the day.
Then up, and straight back down again. Brian Powney, brave and squat.
T.Rex, DMs and scarf on wrist, OK?

Heart On My Sleeve

And then the world was wonderful. Punk rock and Peter Ward!
And sidekick 'Spider' Mellor, tall and lean.
The legendary Walsall game. Promotion. Riding high.
Southampton-Spurs: that stitch-up was obscene.
The final glorious victory. Division One at last!
Arsenal, first game, midst fevered expectation.
Those Highbury gods tore us to shreds; we learned the lesson well.
Steve Foster was our soul and inspiration!

Man City came, and Gerry Ryan waltzed through them to score
And mighty Man United bit the dust.
Notts Forest, and that Williams screamer nearly broke the net.
The Norwich quarter-final: win or bust!
And after Wembley, Liverpool were toppled one last time.
The final curtain on those happy days.
And then the years of gradual, inexorable decline -
sadly for some, the parting of the ways.

But we stayed true, as glory days turned into donkeys' years.
Young, Trusson, Tiltman, Farrington. Ee-aw!
A Wilkins free-kick nearly brought us hope. 'Twas not to be.
The rot was deep and spreading to the core.
We found our voice and Lloyd was gone. Hooray! But worse to come.
Though just how awful we were yet to know.
Dissent turned to rebellion and then to open war
as on the terrace weeds began to grow.

The Goldstone sold behind our backs! Enraged, we rose as one
against a stony northern businessman.
We drew a line, and said: ENOUGH! And as the nation watched
The final battle for our club began.
We fought him to a standstill. Fans United. All for one.
A nation's colours joined: a glorious sight.
And, finally, the stubborn, stony Archer moved his ground
and made way for our own collective Knight.

The battle's only just begun, but we have won the war.
Our club, though torn asunder, will survive.
And I salute each one of you who stood up and said NO!
And fought to keep the Albion alive.
And one day, when our new home's built, and we are storming back
A bunch of happy fans without a care
We'll look back on our darkest hour and raise our glasses high
and say with satisfaction: we were there.

But first we have to face today. The hardest day of all.
Don't worry if you can't hold back the tears!
We must look to the future, in dignity and peace
as well as mourn our home of ninety years.
For me the Goldstone has an extra special memory
of the football soulmate I so briefly had.
He christened me John Charles and taught me to love the game.
This one's for Bill. A poet. And my dad.

1997

FROM HEREFORD TO HERE

Performed on TV before our first ever game in the Premier League in 2017, at home to Man City.

With sheer determination
A vision fine and clear
We made the noise which brought the boys
From Hereford to here.

Mid Nineties. The fightback began.
We met each Monday night
And called for help to save our club.
He answered. Thanks, Dick Knight.
So many colours joined with ours
On Fans United Day
And then we drew at Hereford
And drank the night away.

A joyous celebration
Washed down by lakes of beer -
We made the noise which brought the boys
From Hereford to here.

Homeless. 'Right, Brighton Council.
Find us somewhere to play.
'Cos we're the Seagulls Party now
And we'll vote you away...'

Heart On My Sleeve

Withdean. Bobby Zamora.
We really cut a dash.
He scored the goals which took us up –
I cheered and played the Clash.

With pride and dedication
And not a hint of fear
We made the noise which brought the boys
From Hereford to here.

So welcome, world, to our new home.
It took so Blooming long!
Petitions. Demonstrations.
A Top 20 hit song…
Our lovely Falmer Stadium.
The Board may not agree.
I've never had a credit card.
It's still Falmer to me.

With hope and expectation
And yes, a little tear
We made the noise which brought the boys
From Hereford to here.

Now we're a bunch of fans again
All cheering on our team.
A glorious end to twenty years.
Fulfilment of a dream.
The Albion in the Premier League
And we've all played our part.
We're more than corporate football, us.
We're football's beating heart.

This is our celebration
So have another beer -
We've made the noise and brought the boys
From Hereford
To here.

2017

AND SMITH MUST SCORE
(Brighton & Hove Albion v Manchester United, FA Cup Final, 1983....our finest hour)

Five yards out, an open goal
and not a man in sight
The memory of that awful miss
still haunts me late at night...
Ten seconds left in extra time
and history in the making
but Smith's shot hit the goalie's legs
and now our hearts are breaking.

A paralytic lemming
with the skill of a dead cat
and the finesse of a hamster
could have done better than that...
A decomposing dogfish
wrapped in bondage head to toe
could have stuck that ball into the net
but Gordon Smith? Oh no!

When Robinson broke down the left
and stuck the ball across
we knew for sure the Seagulls' win
was Man United's loss
and as old Smithy shaped to shoot
a mighty roar went up...
The impossible had happened!
We'd won the FA Cup!

A fleeting glimpse of glory -
alas, 'twas not to be...
we lost the replay 4-0
went down to Division Three.
The one chance of a lifetime
so cruelly snatched away
But till the white coats come for me
I'll never forget that day!

1983

ARCHER'S SHAME

They say that he's greedy, corrupt, and a liar -
and they wouldn't pass water on him if afire.
They've disowned him, they hate him, and he is to blame
And everywhere headlines scream out 'Archer's Shame!'
So strangely familiar, this rage and this fuss.
Such memories for each and every one of us
And so right and so fitting that Jeffrey should pay.
But I still can't help thinking, as he's banged away,
though an Archer in prison is justice well done,
that, as foul as he is, they've locked up the wrong one.

1997

A SYMPTOM OF MODERN SOCIETY...

It's a symptom of modern society.
When our team's getting stuffed, we complain!
When our history's sold for developers' gold
We protest again and again!

When we're told we're 'half-wits' who 'make trouble'
We get angry and filled with suspicion.
'Cos behind talk like that there's quite often a rat
Abusing a hallowed position...

We're no longer just dumb cannon fodder.
We're the fans, it's our club, and we care.
We want participation, not patronisation!
Let us in - we'll do more than our share.

Please don't tell us to 'mind our own business'.
It's our 'business' as much as it's yours!
We've been there since the start, we're the lifeblood, the heart.
Ever played a match behind closed doors?

It's a symptom of modern society.
We supporters have got off our knees!
It's a symptom we're going to encourage -
Until it becomes a disease!

2001

THE LEPPINGS LANE END

It looks so different now, but I still recall how
In this place there was horror and fear.
Some people I know simply don't want to go:
I'll be there, and come back every year.
When I'm Hillsborough bound, the same thought comes around
One which caused this short verse to be penned.
The best antidote to that old Shankly quote
Is to stand in the Leppings Lane end.

We all have our dreams and our hopes for our teams
And we sing 'till we die' in our youth.
Those folk sang, then they died. The police and press lied.
It took twenty seven years till the truth.
And if, as they may, Wednesday beat us today
To this comforting thought I'll hold fast.
We'll walk out of the ground and get home safe and sound.
For the 96, justice at last.

2016

TERMS AND CONDITIONS

When our new Chief Executive referred to we fans as 'customers', I wrote this to put him right.

At the meal table, I'm a consumer.
I'm a customer when in a shop.
For the sake of our poor English language
That's where corporate brand-speak should stop.
When I get on a train, I'm a passenger
(And to hell with their privatised plan)
At my gigs, I perform to an audience.
At the Albion, I am a fan.

A consumer will gulp down a product
Till a better one's sold on TV.
A customer's wallet goes elsewhere
If he's not got the right guarantee.
But we fans will be there for a lifetime.
We'll stand up for our rights come what may.
We're the core, we're not passive consumers -
And that's why our club's still here today.

2015

FOR ROY
Roy Chuter, my great friend

Now there are those who walk on by
And there are those who make a stand.
We stood, and you were one of us.
My good mate Roy, at my right hand.

Those BISA meetings, Monday nights.
Bellotti's letter: you had fun!
Through demos, protests, legal fights
We built a bonfire – and we won.

You wrote with wit and style and skill
For Gull's Eye fanzine, programme too.
A pint in hand, a ready word.
You helped to make our dream come true.

A friend for two thirds of my life
Who fought so long our great club's cause.
There in the Albion's darkest hour.
So sad we could not be in yours.

2013

ANOTHER FOOTBALL OBSCENITY
(Written for my Northwich wife, Robina, and for her much loved home town club, the Vics.)

At the end of this season
the oldest football ground of them all
around which whole lives have been built
for a century and a quarter
replete with history
haunted by the ghosts of the past
will be concreted over by soulless moneymen
to save a debt-crippled club from extinction.

The Drill Field.
Home of Northwich Victoria FC.
Football played continuously there since 1874.
The cradle
of the greatest game the world has ever known
- a game which England gave to the world.
It should be cherished.
Preserved for posterity.
The pride of the Football Association.
But no....

There is no history.
Just Champions League. Premiership. Sky TV.
Southerners in Man U shirts
soulless, overpriced all-seater stadia
and more dull tabloid headlines
as another rootless mercenary changes masters for twenty million pounds.
For the rest...
Market forces rule, they say.
Let the bulldozers come.
We know how that feels.
It's unspeakable.

For the record:
Northwich Vics have debts
of £450,000.
Seven week's wages
for Roy Keane.

2002

A PRIDE OF SEAGULLS
Written at the request of the club to welcome the annual Pride celebrations to our city.

You flood our friendly city's streets
In a flamboyant tide
We welcome you and celebrate
The glory that is Pride.

Yes, we can see you holding hands.
It's not that hard to tell!
Your boyfriends know that you are here -
Because they're here as well.

We're in the twenty first century.
It's all quite normal. Yet
Some sing such chants at Brighton fans
And think we'll be upset...

Oh, Oscar Wilde! Such cutting wit!
No need to have them muzzled.
It's far more fun to fling 'em back
And see the morons puzzled.

Thus: 'You're too ugly to be gay'
We sing. They are perplexed.
And 'One nil to the nancy boys'
Just leaves them doubly vexed.

Yes, we are Brighton, from the South.
And most of us will say
Proud of our city and our club -
And proud for you today.

N-N-N-NINE NIL (The Paul Hardcastle Remix!)
Remember Paul Hardcastle's crap disco hit 'N-n-n-nineteen..?'

(For the uninitiated... Brighton fans don't like Crystal Palace!)

Tuesday September 8th 1989 began like any other day in the footballing calendar, with newly-discovered Team of the 80s, Crystal Palace, travelling to Anfield to test their Colditz-like defensive qualities and mesmerising attacking skills against the sacrificial lemmings of Liverpool. Now football is a funny game, as the utterly retarded cliche goes, and on this particular evening it proved to be a very funny game indeed, in fact a positively hilarious, side-splittingly humourous one, even more mirth-inducing than David Beckham trying to define existentialism or Bill Archer attempting coitus with a paper-shredding machine. For while Palace's much-feared rivals Brighton and Hove Albion were thrashing Wolverhampton Wanderers 4-2, at Anfield the final score was Liverpool 9, Crystal Palace 0. Liverpool 9, Crystal Palace 0. N-n-n-nine nil, nine nil. N-n-n-nine nil, nine nil. And following those fateful n-n-n-ninety minutes on that hilarious Tuesday night the hapless halibuts from Selhurst Park were subjected to fierce and merciless ridicule from the rest of the football world and many of them are still living out their experiences to this day. Even now the South London branch of the Samaritans receive mysterious phone calls where the only audible sounds are donkey-like voices braying bewilderedly 'Nine nil. N-n-n-nine nil. Ee-aw! Nine nil. N-n-n-nine nil. Ee-aw! And when the Palace players got home, obviously in need of moral support and counselling following their torrid n-n-n-nine nil experience, none of them received a hero's welcome. None of them. None of them received a hero's welcome. N-n-n-none of them. The long term effects of such an unbelievable n-n-n-nine nil annihilation are hard to predict, but it seems likely that many of the Crystal Palace squad may have been be so demoralised that they may have been forced to leave professional football and sign on. S-s-s-sign on. Sign on. S-s-s-sign on. S-s-s-sign on, sign on. S-s-s-sign on, sign on. A worse fate even than this may well have befallen the Palace goalkeeper Perry Suckling, a man who, rather like the Queen Mother, wears gloves for no apparent reason, for his intense feelings of humiliation may well have led him to emigrate, and sign on in Vietnam. V-v-v-Vietnam. S-s-s-sign on. V-v-v-Vietnam. S-s-s-sign on... (repeat ad nauseam)

SELECTED SONG LYRICS

I say 'selected' and these have very much been: they represent only a small proportion of the songs and melodies I have written in the last 40 years and have been chosen specifically because I think the words work well on the page. All those which I consider to be my finest political songs are here, mainly recorded with my band Barnstormer and chronicling many of the great events of my lifetime: towards the end you will find many of the texts from our 2018 'early music meets punk' historical album 'Restoration Tragedy' dealing with the Levellers, Diggers and Ranters, the radical sects which emerged after the execution of Charles 1 in 1649.

My best known silly songs (eg *Willie Whitelaw's Willy, The Spencers Croft Cat, Doggy on a String*) aren't here. The lyrics really don't work on the page, honestly! Our 2005 Seagulls Ska hit Tom Hark (We Want Falmer) isn't either and many others which will be known to those who have followed my efforts for a fair amount of my 40 years haven't been included for the same reason. Enjoy the recorded versions: if I had included everything I have ever written, poems and songs, this book would be an unliftable brick!

FIFTH COLUMN

1981: riots in Brixton against police brutality and racism. This song foretold how the police would be used as Thatcher's private army in the Miners' Strike three years later.

One Monday night they came along
They told us all to move along
And some, they said, just don't belong
Some just went away
We turned and faced, but they were strong
Riot shield and leather thong
An end to talk of right and wrong:
Who cares now anyway?

The column is the master now
The column on the street
The column in the newspaper
The boot boy on the beat

Every hope destroyed by power
Blackened soot on every flower
Sweetened roses in Madam's bower –
Pleasures that money can buy
Gave us war games to decoy us
Gave us Friedman to destroy us
Education, health deny us
Watch the flowers die

The column is the master now
The column on the street
The column in the newspaper
The boot boy on the beat

Heart On My Sleeve

You'll not quell a people's spirit
It's our war and we will win it
Every second, every minute
Sounds the call to arms
We will gain our resolution
We will find our absolution
In the dustbin, her solution
And her blue rinse charms

Your column will look silly then
Your column on the street
Your column in the Telegraph
The boot boy on the beat
Your column will look ragged then
Your column on the street
Your column in the tabloid press
The boot boy on the beat

And we will not retreat
From the boot boy on the beat
And we will not retreat
From the boot boy on the beat
And we will not retreat
From the boot boy on the beat
And we will not retreat
From the boot boy on the beat
FIFTH COLUMN
FIFTH COLUMN
FIFTH COLUMN
FIFTH COLUMN

SAWDUST AND EMPIRE
Written during the Falklands War, 1982.

On the waterfront they're gathered for the feast
To pay homage to the priestess of the waves
Wider and wider the voices ring out loud
In the celebrating crowd of Albion's braves
But someone told me something that I just don't want to hear
Ancestral words that fooled us for the last six hundred years
But they don't ring true any more

Sawdust and empire - the nectar of the few
So give the devil his due and break away
Sawdust and empire with a hint of royal blue
But I won't drink with you on Empire Day

Dreams of old India, the Bible and the Host
To calm the ghost that won't be laid to rest
A distant island becomes the Holy Grail
In the spirit that revived King Arthur's quest
And you may wear her heraldry in tattoos on your arms
But it takes more than bravado now to soothe old England's qualms
'Cos it don't ring true any more

Sawdust and empire - the nectar of the few
So give the devil his due and break away
Sawdust and empire in the pub and in the pew
But I won't drink with you on empire day

The territories and governors are all gone now
But the bloodlust and the cliches linger on
The territories and governors are all gone now
But the bloodlust and the cliches linger on

Heart On My Sleeve

And in the theatre the fading actor stands
Our destiny a nipple in his hand
And in the Stock Exchange they fly the Union Flag
Though faceless bankers know no motherland
And as I love my country, the harbours and the sea
I will not serve the warmongers who seek my loyalty
'Cos they don't ring true any more

Sawdust and empire - the nectar of the few
So give the devil his due and break away
Sawdust and empire in the pub and in the pew
But I won't drink with you on empire day..

THE BALLAD OF AIRSTRIP ONE

Written on December 31st 1983 as the American Cruise missiles were about to be brought into UK bases. 'Airstrip One' is Orwell's description of the UK as an unsinkable aircraft carrier for a foreign power (from his novel '1984').

Another New Year and too much beer and a puke into the sea
Though the lights of Shoreham Harbour still look the same to me
And some bloke on the radio is saying things that I've heard before
And he's going on about Orwell and it's getting rather a bore
And out there in the darkness there's a Yankee with a gun
But we're too wrecked to care right now 'cos the New Year's just begun
We're having fun
Down on Airstrip One

The Harlow lights shine brightly as the wheels eat up the road
But the motorways are runways now and they're carrying a deadly load
'Cos the monsters are all mobile and there's anarchy in the air
And the driver's name is Sutcliffe and he's too far gone to care
And if you think your Kentish prayers are mightier than the gun
I'll tell you that you're dreaming 'cos the coundown's just begun
But we'll still have fun
Down on Airstrip One

Some folks are angry and some folks are cool
Read all the newspapers, don't be a fool
Video nasties and sugary tea
That's the way to get away scot free
On Airstrip One...

There's some choose civilisation and a promise unfulfilled
And there's some choose extermination – when it's someone else who gets killed
A gesture of insanity and a world left to the crabs
Five thousand years of history and now they're up for grabs
So send that fucking cowboy riding off into the sun
And send with him the culture of the dollar and the gun
Then we'll have fun
Down on Airstrip One

LIBYAN STUDENTS FROM HELL!
Written after the American attack on Libya, 1986.
(The original version of the lyrics. There have been many...)

Just look at us - we're the scourge of the land
We're Colonel Gadaffi's favourite band
We all eat babies and we're commies too
And we've all got AIDS and we'll give it to you
With scaly tails and horns and hooves
We undermine everything that moves
You can read about us in the right wing press
The Sun, the Mail and the Express
So don't mess with us, cos we're foreign and we smell -
We're the Libyan Students from Hell!

If your telly goes wrong or your car won't start
You can bet your life that we played our part
If your team doesn't win or you miss the bus
Then ten to one it was down to us
If a dog runs off with your copy of the Sun
And brings it back with the crossword done
If someone smacks you in the head
Or you find a terrapin in your bed
we did it - and everything else as well
Cos we're Libyan Students from Hell!

There's nothing very prudent
About a Libyan student
Can't you tell?
There's nothing very prudent
About a Libyan student
From Hell!

Attila The Stockbroker

We imported Neighbours to these shores
We personally started both World Wars
We broke your Gran's Coronation mugs
We sold Ben Johnson all his drugs
We caused the Plague and the Great Fire too
and we brought 'The Price Is Right' to you
We pushed Robert Maxwell over the side
We took Marc Bolan for his last ride
So don't mess with us 'cos we're foreign and we smell
We're the Libyan Students from Hell...

MARKET SEKTOR ONE

Written in 1990 on my first return to East Germany after the Wall had come down, having done four tours under 'actually existing socialism'. A song supporting the movement for a free, independent GDR and opposing unification. The German language version I sing has been covered by two German bands, which makes me very proud. And, yes, it uses the same tune as 'The Ballad of Airstrip One'. (The only time I've ever done this.)

Another new year and too much beer and goodbye to the Wall
But now there's only disappointment, nothing left at all
The dreams we marched and fought for have faded and turned sour
The cabbage is a king now, it's Helmut's finest hour
And on the streets the people want it 'as seen on TV'
And a big bunch of bananas is a sign that you are 'free'
It's just begun – Market Sektor One

As in the East we talk about a future bold and new
A thousand Western businessmen are celebrating too
The vultures are all circling, there is money to be made
A multinational carve up, a bank to be obeyed
And now the old, rich foreigners make claims on every hand -
'You're living in my house, mein Herr, you're farming on my land'
It's time to run – Market Sektor One

Is that all that we were fighting for?
Bananas and sex shops, nothing more?
Welcome to the Western dream
Welcome to the cheap labour scheme

The whole of Europe's changing – Big Brother's on the run
It could just be a whole new age of freedom has begun
But freedom doesn't bow its head to some financier's will
And Europe is our common home, not some gigantic till
So send the money grabbers riding off into the sun
And send with them the culture of the dollar and the gun
Then we'll have fun
And justice will be done…

TYLER SMILES
Written after the 1990 Peasants' Revolt against Thatcher's Poll Tax, looking back at the previous one in 1381...

Here's to you, the sceptic few
In the dark old days of '82
When a thousand corpses stoked an awful pyre
Here's to '84 and 5
When all our dreams took another dive
'Midst the jeers of Mammon and the howls of the Digger's choir
There were times I really thought
They'd all been conned and all been bought
Too much Chingford on the brain
And never going to think again
But it's a taxing time for Essex now

And Tyler smiles, Tyler smiles
On an angry crowd stretching miles and miles
Six hundred years but the lesson wasn't learned
And Tyler smiles, Tyler smiles
Though a hail of bricks and stones and tiles
Now history rolls back, the worm has turned
Retribution earned

Tell me why it took so long
All these years we've sung this song -
And will the spectre ever go away?
A hundred thousand garden gnomes
Outside a hundred thousand homes
Are 'standing on their own two feet' today
No strident tones now, just a whine
A hand picked bank clerk holds the line
The same song with a few new chords
For Albion's user-friendly hordes
A thornless rose is flopping in the breeze

Heart On My Sleeve

And Tyler smiles, Tyler smiles
Through the acid rain and the sheepdog trials -
Perhaps he never really went away
And Tyler smiles, Tyler smiles
On the village greens and the seven dials
There's still a bit of fight in us today...
Tyler smiles.

And if it's really over
And the swords turn into ploughshares
She'll go to Eastern Europe -
Oh, they really love her there
The fool Walesa and the iron curse

And Tyler smiles, Tyler smiles
As Labour's leaders close their files
On 'Wat's his name?' from their own history
And Tyler smiles, Tyler smiles
On that angry crowd stretching miles and miles
'Hey, gotcha, lady, gotcha - finally!'
Tyler smiles.

THIS IS FREE EUROPE

Probably my best known anti-fascist song.
Originally written in 1991, revised many times since.

Dead of night in Carpentras
Brings the ghosts from the days of Vichy
Broken windows in the high street
Swastikas in the cemetery
Blond young men on a Rostock evening
Beer and loathing on their breath
Ten to one like their cowardly fathers
Arms outstretched in the sign of death

If it takes a voice then shout the truth
If it takes a hand then hold them back
If it takes a fist then smash them down
From Cable Street to Hoyerswerda
Griffin, Schonhuber and Le Pen -
This is Free Europe! Never again!

Afternoon in a Russian city
Now they don't even need to hide
Blueshirt thugs advertise their pogroms
None are arrested, none are tried
'Pamyat' means 'a memory'-
What memories for these Russian Nazis?
Children killed in front of their mothers
Human skin turned into lampshades

If it takes a voice then shout the truth
If it takes a hand then hold them back
If it takes a fist then smash them down
From Cable Street to Hoyerswerda
Griffin, Schonhuber and Le Pen -
This is Free Europe! Never again!

Heart On My Sleeve

Once more we see the darkness in the European soul
As the chains fall, there comes an awful beast
His eyes are staring, and there is hell upon his brow:
Oskar, Francois, Gregor, Tanya, listen to me now...

If it takes a voice then shout the truth
If it takes a hand then hold them back
If it takes a fist then smash them down
From Cable Street to Hoyerswerda
Griffin, Schonhuber and Le Pen -
This is Free Europe! Never again!

I'm a Jew in Carpentras
I'm a Jew in a Russian city
I'm an Asian in the East End
I'm a Cuban in East Germany
Don't tell me it doesn't concern us
It's not something to ignore
They are feeding on our apathy:
That's how it began before...

If it takes a voice then shout the truth
If it takes a hand then hold them back
If it takes a fist then smash them down
From Cable Street to Hoyerswerda
Griffin, Schonhuber and Le Pen -
This is Free Europe! Never again!

SARAJEVO
Written during the Yugoslav Civil War, 1994
Dedicated to Laibach

You don't have to sit back and watch psychopaths fight
The hand of friendship is usually right
Most people want peace and a home somewhere
They don't care about the thugs and their murderous stare
Now we knew this and for forty years
A brand new way replaced traditional fears
Most people lived happily side by side
No place for terror, no need to hide
But it wasn't to the liking of the World Bank suits
Who cheered as the tribes rediscovered their roots
They can handle torture, rape and death
If it opens up markets for the IMF

And they're 'free' now, oh they're 'free' now
'A chance for individuals to compete'
'Free' now, oh they're 'free' now
Fascists gun down children in the street

I remember the messages from Amnesty
Which said the whole damned lot of them should be 'free'
No matter what they say, no matter what they do
Cos they're 'all entitled to their point of view'
The liberals cheered when the moneymen won
Now they cry in the face of the tank and the gun
And the arms manufacturers are having fun as well
Growing fat on the profits of sectarian hell
Now Tito saw it another way
For a hundred years educate each day
And suppress the thugs and their murderous lie
Keep the lid on the pot till the hate boiled dry

But they're 'free' now, oh they're 'free' now
The rape camp guards can have a Big Mac for tea
'Free' now, oh they're 'free' now
Welcome to Western liberal democracy

There's 'freedom' in Bischofferode in East Germany
A town closed due to 'economic unviability'
The word has become meaningless, a travesty
For there can be no freedom without power for the free
... and that means more than shopping, actually

In Afghanistan in 1979
Everybody swallowed the American line
Misogynists from the eighth century
Were 'freedom fighters' on TV
Kabul was intact, there was peace in the air
A new society was being built there
Then the terrorists attacked in Allah's name
Though they were playing the corporate game
Taliban stooges for American cash
Put women under veil and lash
And when they bit the hand that fed
Bin Laden escaped and the innocent bled

They're 'free' now, oh they're 'free' now
They starve in Moscow, burn in Chechnya
They're 'free' now, oh, they're 'free' now
Fascism, war, poverty, mafia
They're 'free' now, oh, they're 'free' now
Look 'freedom' up in the latest dictionary
'Free' now, oh, they're 'free' now
It says: an IMF loan and a monetarist economy

In East Berlin the satirists sing
'Auf die Dauer hilft nur Mauer
We want our wall back, we want our wall back
Can we have our wall back please?'

MOHAMMED THE KABUL RED

While the US Government were busy bankrolling the fundamentalist lunatics who would end up attacking the World Trade Center, I wrote this in the style of the Ramones. 'PDPA' means 'People's Democratic Party of Afghanistan' by the way.

Here's a song about a man
Leftist in Afghanistan
Fought against the Taliban
When their backers were American

New way for Afghanistan
Radical, secular programme
Woman liberated, equal to man
But that didn't suit the American...

Mohammed the Kabul Red
Fought bin Laden all the way
Mohammed the Kabul Red
Member of the PDPA

Taliban funded by the CIA
Bin Laden trained by the CIA
Terrorists supported by the CIA
Medieval thugs in Washington's pay...

Mohammed tortured, hung in the street
Woman stoned for showing her feet
White House says - 'Job's complete!
Now we've got those Commies beat!'

Mohammed the Kabul Red
Fought bin Laden all the way
Mohammed the Kabul Red
Member of the PDPA

Terrorists strike - fire and flame
And bin Laden gets the blame
Trade Centre bombed, American tears
So why did they fund him for over ten years?

Here's a song about a man
Leftist in Afghanistan
Fought against the Taliban
When their backers were American

Mohammed the Kabul Red
Fought bin Laden all the way
Mohammed the Kabul Red
Member of the PDPA
P-D-PDPA
P-D-PDPA
P-D-PDPA
P-D-PDPA

THE BLANDFORD FORUM

Inspired by Blair's trip to Australia to beg for Rupert Murdoch's support in the 1997 General Election.

Our voice is still, our memories subside
A dream of quiet nothing spurs us on
Canute floats out to sea, then back in with the tide
Our hopes and expectations are long gone
Cries of Pyrrhic victory fade into a snore
As a freshly laundered cockroach crawls across the panelled floor

Hold the front page, light the lamp –
there's a new face in the Labour camp
Talking of a slightly better day
Forged the thumbscrews, worked the racks,
cracked the whip across our backs
Now he's turned a pinker shade of grey…

The boundaries set in stone along the Walworth Road
Leave wit and anger voiceless at the door
The land is bland, the wan-eyed man is king
And so shall be for now and evermore
This is England, dear old England, beloved unto me:
Land of dope and Tory, single mother of the free

Hold the front page, light the lamp –
there's a new face in the Labour camp
Flew to Oz to find a Holy Grail
Rupert rules so sell your soul:
Procol Harum protocol
Let's all turn a whiter shade of pale

Like plaice in the sand of Shoreham
They change to suit the tide
While the Laird of the Blandford Forum
Takes our history for a ride
(But it's what the customer wants…)

Heart On My Sleeve

When Burnham Wood sprouts over Dunsinane
And Seagulls fly unhindered through the year
Canute will build a dam that's not made out of sand
While publicans serve hogsheads of free beer
When we build a Wapping fire to blacken out the Sun
Every Midas in the midden will be on the chicken run....

Hold the front page, light the lamp
There's a new face in the labour camp
Actually, it seems there's quite a few
Some might say it's a bit unfair
I say we should leave them there
'Til they turn a redder shade of blue

Hold the front page, light the lamp
There's a new face in the labour camp

SCUMBALL PINOCHET

Written in 1999 when Thatcher invited the Chilean dictator over for tea, reflecting on the injustice of life – my childhood rock n roll hero Marc Bolan died at 29 and that fascist murdering scumbag lived to be 91. An anti-fascist song in the style of T.Rex, and a pun on the T.Rex song 'Spaceball Ricochet'.

One wrote songs that meant a lot to me
but his partner wrapped a Mini round a sycamore tree
and the other one was evil fascist torturing scum
but he lived to over ninety – the Reaper wouldn't come

Scumball Pinochet should have got a ricochet
20th Century Boy should still be getting it on today

One met his Metal Guru at the age of twenty nine
While the other one grew old on torture and wine
It's sixty years too short and it's eighty years too long
and the Children Of The Revolution think it's wrong!

Scumball Pinochet should have got a ricochet
20th Century Boy should still be getting it on today

They both had their heyday in 1973
One was The Groover who Loved To Boogie
The other killed thousands of people in Chile
And he lived to be old – that's really bloody silly...

And the message from the government's the really last straw
that a killer aged eighty's not a killer any more
But one way or another he's gone to meet his fate
And Telegram Sam says hell can't wait...

Scumball Pinochet should have got a ricochet
20th Century Boy should still be getting it on today

BICYCLE TESTICLE

Marc Bolan was known for nonsensical rhyming song titles ('Telegram Sam', 'Pewter Suitor', 'Salamanda Palaganda') and equally nonsensical but beautiful lyrics, often containing 'ows'. This is my tribute to his style and happened after I sustained a minor cycling injury.

Ow ow ow
Ow ow ow
Bicycle testicle ow
Bicycle testicle ow

Bicycle-sore testicle, wrapped in ancient silk
Damaged by the black clad poet drunk on narwhal's milk
Wrinkled like the crags of Albion, cloaked in curls of maize
Destined for to dangle swollen 'neath my lady's gaze

Bicycle testicle ow
Bicycle testicle ow

Hirsute orb of mystery where future souls are grown
Gainst crossbar of destiny like Icarus was thrown
Folds of puckish damask crushed on heartless steel of Fate
Poet begs the metal guru: make the pain abate

Bicycle testicle ow
Bicycle testicle ow
Ow ow ow
Ow ow ow

2020

JUST ONE LIFE
Written for my wife-to-be Robina in 1999

Here is a celebration for a lifetime
Bang on the jackpot, straight out of the blue
Awestruck with love and a simple recognition
Two halves united, the perfect team in action, me and you

Just one life

This is year zero, welcome to the future
Here in each each other we've found eternity
When I returned to my piece of Smalltown England
I must have known you were waiting here for me - it had to be

Just one life

No more compromise and no more pain
Everything is different now - we are the same

Put up and shut up never quelled your spirit
Dustbin of history is where they now belong
We're the collective - we will stand together
Fasten your seatbelt and take my hand –
the empty years have gone

Just one life that's all we get so no faint hearts and no regret
Savour the moment, live every day, seize the dream when it comes your way
Just one life
Bigots and hypocrites can all get lost, it's time to defrost
Preach, preach, preach to the rebel
Deep in the rainforest
In the heart of the bush…
Roots rock rebel!

DEATH OF A SALESMAN
Written just after the attack on the World Trade Center, September 11th, 2001

You were there in Chile, 11 September '73
Twenty eight years to the day - what a dreadful irony
Victor Jara singing 'midst the tortured and the dead
White House glasses clinking as Allende's comrades bled...

You were there in '79 in the hills above Kabul
Teaching a bunch of psychopaths the fastest way to kill
Just pawns in your global strategy, another little right wing war
But now you reap just what you sow - the monster's at the door

And you don't understand why those people are so angry
And you don't understand why they don't go shopping too
And you don't understand why your garish colours blind them
Dismiss, exploit and bully - then you wonder at their hate
So many cruel deaths
But these are different, these are American
Now death counts - death of a salesman

You use the world as your sweatshop on a bare subsistence wage
Then along come medieval murderers to exploit the people's rage
And Europe takes the profits too, then grovels on its knees
Saying 'after you, you rule the world, so do just as you please'

And you don't understand why those people are so hungry
And you don't understand why they don't go shopping too
And you don't understand why your garish colours blind them
Dismiss, exploit and bully - then you wonder at their hate
So many cruel deaths
But these are different, these are American
Now death counts - death of a salesman

Attila The Stockbroker

We don't need your religion, whether Allah, money or God
We won't cheer on your armies, won't wield your avenging rod
We stand for justice, for the future,
For the millions of women and men
Who see through the lies and work for the day
When sanity rules again

And you don't understand why those people are so angry
And you don't understand why they don't go shopping too
And you don't understand why your garish colours blind them
Dismiss, exploit and bully - then you wonder at their hate
So many cruel deaths
But these are different, these are American
Now death counts - death of a salesman

HEY CELEBRITY!
I am an advocate of celebricide. Not of the individuals, obviously. Of the concept.

Hey, celebrity! TV bore!
What have you done to be famous for?
Hey, celebrity! Tabloid whore!
What do people need you for...?

Once again the headlines shout
I don't know what they're on about
I've got my own life, don't need yours
Use TV for the teletext scores
Why do they need you, what do they see?
I don't need you, I'm happy with me
Millions and millions of women and men
Watching you again and again
Talking 'bout you, again and again
Living through you, again and again...

Hey, celebrity! TV bore!
What have you done to be famous for?
Hey, celebrity! Tabloid whore!
What do people need you for?

Brain dead TV soap, Big Brother
Shepherds for the sheep one way or the other
Celebrity diets, celebrity dress
Celebrity trivia, celebrity press
One day one of you said to me
'Hey, Attila that's what you want to be
All your talk's just jealousy
You just wanna be like me
You just wanna live like me
Wanna be famous just like me
Wanna be famous just like me.....'

But hey, celebrity! TV bore!
What have you done to be famous for?
Hey, celebrity! Tabloid whore!
What do people need you for?

Why do they all want this stuff?
Why aren't their own lives more than enough?
We've so much to see and do
We've no time to waste on you....
Hardly ever watch TV
Read the news selectively
You're on telly, in the tabloids too
We're not interested in you!
We're not interested in you!
We're not interested in you!
We're not interested in you!

Hey, celebrity! TV bore!
What have you done to be famous for?
Hey, celebrity! Tabloid whore!
What do people need you for?
What do people need you for?
What do people need you for?

2004

COMANDANTE JOE
(Dedicated to the memory of Joe Strummer, 1952-2002)

I guess in quite a lot of ways I grew up just like you
A bolshy kid who didn't think the way they told him to
You kicked over the statues, a roots rock rebel star
Who knew that punk was more than just the sound of a guitar
And I'll always remember that night at the Rainbow
When you wrote a soundtrack for my life,
Comandante Joe.

So many bands back then were like too many bands today
A bunch of blokes who made a noise with bugger all to say
The Clash were always out in front, you put the rest to shame
Your words were calls to action, your music was a flame
You were our common Dante, and you raised an inferno
And you wrote a soundtrack for my life,
Comandante Joe.

Reggae in the Palais
Midnight till six!
Rockin' Reds in Brockwell Park!
Sten guns in Knightsbridge!
Up and down the Westway
In and out the lights!
Clash City Rockers!
Know Your Rights!

I guess in quite a lot of ways I grew up just like you
A bolshy kid who didn't think the way they told him to
Like you I always knew that words and music held the key
As you did for so many, you showed the way to me
Although I never met you, I'm so sad to see you go
'Cos you wrote a soundtrack for my life,
Comandante Joe.

2002

GUY FAWKES' TABLE

Written on March 19th 2003, the first full day after the vote by a Labour Government the night before to support Bush's illegal war in Iraq. I was on tour and I'd gone for a pint in the Mother Shipton Inn by Mother Shipton's Cave in Knaresborough. When I sat down with my drink, I saw a plaque on the table in front of me. 'This table belonged to Guy Fawkes during his time in Knaresborough' it read. I wrote this song in the next twenty minutes.

I'm sitting at Guy Fawkes' table
The day Parliament voted for war
Though the mass of the people opposed it
And it flouts international law
I'm sitting at Guy Fawkes' table
While American thugs flaunt their power
Egged on by a sad little muppet
And his craven and cowardly shower

Aneurin Bevan, your party is dead
And the time for a new one is nigh
Will the last person Left please turn out the lights?
New Labour, just fuck off and die!

They won't be caught up in the carnage
They'll be pontificating right here
Their kids won't be Iraqi conscripts
Moved down while they're shitting with fear
Saddam was the Yanks' chosen ally
On a whim, they now say he must fall
So they'll carpet bomb defenceless soldiers -
But that's not 'mass destruction' at all....

Aneurin Bevan, your party is dead
And the time for a new one is nigh
Will the last person Left please turn out the lights?
New Labour, just fuck off and die!

Heart On My Sleeve

I'm sitting at Guy Fawkes' table
As Bush and his muppet connive
And I'm filled with unspeakable anger
And I'm thinking of 1605
One message, Dishonourable Members
Who endorsed an illegal attack -
No, I don't want to bomb you like Guy did
But I'd love to send you to Iraq!

Aneurin Bevan, your party is dead
And the time for a new one is nigh
Will the last person Left please turn out the lights?
New Labour, just fuck off and die!

We need a new socialist party -
But not the Judean People's Front
Not another small sect, but a movement
With the power to change and confront
We need an electoral system
Which gives every voter a voice
'Cos we're fed up with voting for traitors
And we have the right to a choice!

Aneurin Bevan, your party is dead
And the time for a new one is nigh
Will the last person Left please turn out the lights?
New Labour, just fuck off and die!

BAGHDAD SKA

Hooray Hooray for the USA!
Your soldiers took Saddam away
So we're going out on the streets to play
And celebrate our liberation day
The hospitals overflow with dead
The looters have stolen all the bread
But I think my family are all OK
And you said this was the only way
You said this was the only way

I saw an old friend the very next day
Armed to the teeth and up for the fray
He said 'I'll make those Yankees pay!'
- A B52 blew his wife away
I put my hand upon his head
I held him close and softly said
'I know it's an awful price to pay'
Then sadly I went on my way
Sadly I went on my way

This is Baghdad's scar
This is Baghdad ska
This is Baghdad's scar
This is Baghdad ska

Walked up to a Yankee yesterday
Asked how long they were going to stay
And how he'd reply to the folks who say
Our land was stolen by the USA
Then a shot rang out from across the road
I stood and watched his head explode
And all I could do was cringe and pray
As boots and fists took me away
Boots and fists took me away

Heart On My Sleeve

This is Baghdad's scar
This is Baghdad ska
This is Baghdad's scar
This is Baghdad ska

They're gonna take me to Guantanamo Bay
An enemy of the USA
They don't believe a word I say
They sneer that I'm in for a very long stay
I cry my own, my country's tears
How many dead, how many years?
And through my agony I say:
There could have been another way
There should have been another way

This is Baghdad's scar
This is Baghdad ska
This is Baghdad's scar
This is Baghdad ska

2003

VALENTINE'S DAY
A true story, 2003

I said come, we'll make it special, and here we are, Valentine's Day
In a wild impetuous journey up the M1 motorway
In my boots and Rancid sweatshirt I'll try hard to cut a dash
And I'll serenade you, darling, with Hans Blix and the Clash

Now you say I'm not romantic, but you know I can beguile
That daffodil was dead - but oh, presented with such style!
A bindweed flower buttonhole, some earrings with panache
And hours and hours of traffic jams with Hans Blix and the Clash

There's war news on the radio
Joe Strummer on the stereo
And something happening down below
That no-one else can see
Another town, another show
But always I need you to know
You make me think and make me grow
The other half of me

Here's to us, our great adventure,
and to you, my darling wife
I will stand so proud beside you
through the ups and downs of life
As your fingers do the walking
I will try hard not to crash
And I'll bring us safe to Sheffield
with Hans Blix and The Clash

Two songs inspired by the aftermath of the 'financial crash' of 2008....

LOOTERS

Dazza is a looter
In trainers and a hood
He trashed his local corner shop
He'd learned that greed is good
The CCTV nailed him
The papers called him scum
Now Dazza's in the barry place
Crying for his mum

There's no such thing as society
So steal and cheat and loot
Just one thing to remember though -
Make sure you wear a suit!

Bazza is a looter
In pinstripe, brogues and tie
Short selling in the City
He made millions on the sly
He nicked our hard earned savings
Then turned round and said thanks
He walked off with the money -
We bailed out the banks!

There's no such thing as society
So steal and cheat and loot
Just one thing to remember though -
Make sure you wear a suit!

When greed's the creed that breeds and breeds
What else can you expect?
The selfish scum get richer
And communities get wrecked
Some rob us with an iron bar
Some a computer screen
And when they say it's 'legal'
it's even more obscene...

Dazza is a street kid
And what he did was wrong
But he probably wouldn't do it
If he felt he could belong
Bazza's rich and privileged
He doesn't give a shit
He takes us for a load of mugs
And gets away with it!

There's no such thing as society
So steal and cheat and loot
Just one thing to remember though -
Make sure you wear a suit!

BYE BYE BANKER

They say we've got to keep a hold of all our bankers
'Cos they're so clever and so talented you know
And if we don't give them their bonuses of millions
Then they'll just pick up their briefcases and go
Well they're so clever that they bankrupted the country
And they're so talented our taxes bailed them out
And the government is frightened by their puny little threats
But the rest of us just wanna scream and shout:

Go, go, just sod off now and go
But you can all leave your passports at the door
And the same goes for your houses, your money and your cars
'Cos you're not welcome in this country any more

Well they gamble with our money on the markets
Which is not the function of a bank at all
And they're paid a hundred times more than someone who saves lives
It's time we dealt with this once and for all
I say let's tax them till their testicles are tiny
And make their bonuses some tickets for some planes
And then we'll show the world how we can get along just fine
Without their talented, enormous superbrains

Go, go, just sod off now and go
But you can all leave your passports at the door
And the same goes for your houses, your money and your cars
'Cos you're not welcome in this country any more

But the government is friends with all the bankers
Like Karl Marx predicted all those years ago
And although they caused the mess they've got stooges in the press
Who are desperate to keep the status quo
So the City boys get richer by the hour
While all we get are sackings and cutbacks
And they're brutalising Greece with their IMF police
Yes, it's time to grab those Goldmen by their Sachs!

Attila The Stockbroker

Go, go, just sod off now and go
But you can all leave your passports at the door
And the same goes for your houses, your money and your cars
'Cos you're not welcome in this country any more

We already own some banks, well that's a good start
All we need to do is nationalise the rest
Make the banks work for the people, not the other way around
Put the speculators all under arrest
And as they queue to leave this country for the last time
If they dare to moan or whine or give it large
Tell 'em they're lucky they're not stitching bloody mailbags
'Cos they would be if Attila was in charge...

MISSION CREEP

Written during the brutalisation of Libya by the West in 2011, which – as I predicted in the song – far from leading to democracy, has turned the country into a lawless charnelhouse and breeding ground for Islamic extremism.

I usually cheer at the word 'revolution'
And rebels in action are my kith and kin
But when they are backed by the whole New World Order
That kind of description soon wears pretty thin
Royalists, Islamists, old regime turncoats
Internal divisions already exposed
The flag that they wave is the flag of King Idris
The sad Western toady Gaddafi deposed

No revolution is fronted by NATO
Endorsed by BP, Haliburton and Shell
Businessmen vying to cash in on carnage
Arms dealers profiting, trading in hell

They've not much in common with Chavez or Castro
They're not like the rebels I've cheered on before
Racialist pogroms, massacred prisoners –
I think of the Rebs in the Yank Civil War
Royalty smiles as the old scores are settled
West and Islam in a cynical tryst
Upstart from the desert gets bombed to oblivion
Syrian dynasty slapped on the wrist

No revolution is fronted by NATO
Endorsed by BP, Haliburton and Shell
Businessmen vying to cash in on carnage
Arms dealers profiting, trading in hell

And it's not just the Right who support NATO's actions
'Protecting civilians' - a sick, evil lie
As Sirte is dismantled with bomb and with bullet
Liberals are silent and innocents die
Selective coverage in all the media
One side are heroes, the other side scum
Legitimate targets for air strikes and war crimes –
Now they've been butchered the vultures will come

No revolution is fronted by NATO
Endorsed by BP, Haliburton and Shell
Businessmen vying to cash in on carnage
Arms dealers profiting, trading in hell....

This is not mission creep, it's mission control
Another excuse for an oil hungry war
Taxpayers shellng out over a billion
To take out the weapons sold not long before
Bailouts for the bankers, blank cheques for the arms dealers
Poor and the sick and the vulnerable pay
Cameron likes rebels - when they're in Libya
I'm with the rebels here in the UK

No revolution is fronted by NATO
Endorsed by BP, Haliburton and Shell
Businessmen vying to cash in on carnage
Arms dealers profiting, trading in hell

Now the flag of Al Qaeda flies over Benghazi
Foundation of justice is Sharia law
For women, the spectre of veil and polygamy -
Is that what those thousands of airstrikes were for?

ONLY FOOTBALL

His forebears were the butchers on the field at Peterloo
They led the charge and cut the people down
They ruled the mill, starved weavers out, beat Chartists black and blue
Made millions in some hellish sweatshop town
I'm sure he cursed his countrymen in '84 and '5
His queen called them 'the enemy within'
He's the overseer, the usurer, drone within the hive
Whose wallet is his god, his kith and kin

And don't tell me it's only football

His system defines 'ownership' – a mess of paper shares
A slick deal, a commodity acquired
He pulls the strings and works the law so he controls the 'wares'
Then laughs at all the anguish he's inspired
Now we are many thousands, and he is only one
But law and state hold him in their embrace
What kind of law, what kind of state condones what he has done?
A state where social justice has no place

So don't tell me it's only football

And above all, friends, don't tell me please
That it's nothing to do with years of sleaze
The shattered lives and the corporate trough
Don't tell me it's just a sad one-off
That it's nothing to do with politics
That politics and sport don't mix
Don't tell me it's just bad luck
And don't tell me it's only football

Our grounds rose up near stations in old Victorian times
Most urban centres then were barely towns
Built for our teams, then left in trust to us across the years
By folk who loved the game and not just pounds
The vulture sees the soaring price of inner city land
An ailing club which he can desecrate

Attila The Stockbroker

To us it's pride and history, the story of our lives
To him it's just some prime site real estate

So don't tell me it's only football

And above all, friends, don't tell me please
That it's nothing to do with years of sleaze
The shattered lives and the corporate trough
Don't tell me it's just a sad one-off
That it's nothing to do with politics
That politics and sport don't mix
Don't tell me it's just bad luck
And don't tell me it's only football

Our culture has been colonised, our heritage is sold
And moneymen control our national game
It's devil take the hindmost, all hail the Premier League
And if you can't compete, well, that's a shame
There's a superstore development and it's coming to your ground
A pinstriped butcher's waiting with his knife
That butcher struck at my club – he must never strike again
Let's kick him out – of football, and of life!

So don't tell me it's only football

And above all, friends, don't tell me please
That it's nothing to do with years of sleaze
The shattered lives and the corporate trough
Don't tell me it's just a sad one-off
That it's nothing to do with politics
That politics and sport don't mix
Don't tell me it's just bad luck
And don't tell me it's only football
Don't tell me it's only football
Don't tell me it's only football
Because it isn't only football

2011

PRIDE'S PURGE

Mandatory deselection of MPs as it was done in 1648 - a very topical subject at the moment, and with good reason! 'The Rump' is the Rump Parliament: the name given to the MPs who agreed to try Charles I for high treason and were therefore allowed by Pride to keep their seats in the House...

Respect to the MPs who serve the people well
But the greedy and corrupt can all rot in hell
Back in 1648 one man barred the door
Sleazy puppets of the king not welcome any more

Pride's Purge!

Lobbyists for healthcare firms
Out to make a million
Call a halt to PFI –
Remember Carillion!
Sexist pigs with wandering hands
Guzzling in the trough
All their names upon a list
Time to say 'Enough!'

Pride's Purge!
Power to the Rump!

This job is public service
And that you should remember
So watch just where you poke your Dishonourable Member
Or you'll face deselection
Perhaps a stint inside
Time for a reenactment
Remember Thomas Pride

And Pride's Purge!
Power to the Rump...

2018

WELLINGBOROUGH & WIGAN

My sequel to Leon Rosselson's song about the Diggers of 1649.
Many people were inspired by Gerrard Winstanley's call to action.

The king had been beheaded, the world turned upside down
Winstanley and the Diggers cried 'The poor shall wear the crown!'
They made their stand in Surrey upon St George's Hill
But Winstanley was Wigan born, folk there will tell you still
The poverty around him burned deep into his soul
He grew up watching local folk dig common land for coal
That's where he got his digging from, his modern comrades say
And there's a Diggers' Festival in Wigan to this day

It wasn't just in Surrey they were diggin'
This song goes out to Wellingborough and Wigan

The Wellingborough Diggers were inspired to have a go
They said 'all things in common' and on common land did sow
The field there was called Bareshank but it soon was bearing fruit
Till thugs hired by the rich arrived to trample and uproot
The Diggers' manifesto came from teachings by the Church
But priests just served the propertied and left them in the lurch
Although it was so long ago their statement still rings true
And there's a Diggers' Festival in Wellingborough too

It wasn't just in Surrey they were diggin'
This song goes out to Wellingborough and Wigan

Across the South and Midlands on bits of common land
Thirty-four communities in total took a stand
They made appeals to Cromwell but all fell on deaf ears
Their cries for justice drowned out by the cruel landowners' jeers
They echo down the centuries as we campaign today
Against the men of property who hold us in their sway
So many empty houses, so many folk in need
Extremes of wealth and poverty, and profiteers, and greed

It wasn't just in Surrey they were diggin'
This song goes out to Wellingborough and Wigan

2018

ABIEZER COPPE

When myself, the late, great Seething Wells, Little Brother, Joolz and Benjamin Zephaniah started performing our poetry on stage in the early 1980s we called ourselves 'Ranters' after the 17th Century radicals of the same name. Here's the story of their legendary leader.

Now I have been a Ranter for nearly forty years
I've done over three thousand gigs and drunk a lot of beers
Sometimes I have ranted and then partied till I drop -
But I'm a total lightweight next to Abiezer Coppe

Abiezer was a Ranter back in 1649
When he heard Charles had lost his head he drank his weight in wine
He shouted 'Top is bottom, and bottom shall be top!'
Then he got his knob out, Abiezer Coppe

The Puritans were in control but he showed them his arse
He drank and smoked and stood up for the poorest of his class
Declaiming 'God's inside you, and all the rest is plop.
Your church is your local pub!' said Abiezer Coppe

He stood beside the Diggers as they ploughed in the mud
He vowed the Burford Martyrs would be avenged in blood
Made rude songs out of psalms and bawled them out non stop
Then danced round naked with his friends, Abiezer Coppe

To all the godly Puritans he was a ghastly sore
 Polygamy and orgies and blasphemy and more
And even by our standards he was way over the top
But he got loads of followers, Abiezer Coppe

Winstanley and the Diggers disowned him one by one
But he and his bold ranting crew continued to have fun
Till Fairfax sent the troopers round to finally put a stop
And into Newgate Prison tumbled Abiezer Coppe

Some say that he recanted there, I am not so sure
But one thing is for certain - he ranted no more
And for the next few centuries historians gave the chop
To the bold tale of the Ranters and Abiezer Coppe

Then came the 1980s and our punk rock poet crew
We called ourselves the Ranters and we raised a ballyhoo
But though we were loud and beery and all over the shop
We were sober and polite compared to Abiezer Coppe!

2018

THE FISHERMAN'S TALE
While writing the 'Restoration Tragedy' album I dreamed that Charles II's 1651 escape from Shoreham Harbour - across the road from us - was my fault!

My name is John, a fisherman
From Southwick by the sea
And it was in my sleep one night
This story came to me
Now well you know we fishing folk
Our tall tales love to sing
I dreamed I travelled back in time
And nearly caught a king!

I'd tried my luck from Shoreham Port
Along the eastern quay
That banks the River Adur
Then had a pint or three
In the Schooner and the Welly
(Though they weren't built back then)
And as I staggered home I saw
Some shady-looking men

Now one was tall and swarthy
I recognised his face
I rushed to wake the Roundhead troops
As fast as I could race
'Cos in our little harbour
There right before my eyes
I'd seen the royal traitor
Board Tattersall's 'Surprise'!

My feet were all a tangle
My mind a tangle too
I'd had a Revelation
(Or ten. A lovely brew...)
I shouted out 'It's Charles –
He's on Tattersall's ship!'
But they just said 'You're pissed, John –
Go home and have a kip!'

Now I'm a proper Leveller
A mate of Winstanley
But that night in my slumbering thoughts
The beer had levelled me
I couldn't get my words out
I'm glad I'm happily wed
'Cos my wife came and cuddled me
And took me home to bed…

I woke up the next morning
Head aching, mouth agape
And soon the news was everywhere
About the royal escape
'You stupid bloody pisshead!'
Said someone with a kick
'If you'd had five pints fewer
He'd be in Shoreham nick!'

My name is John, a fisherman
From Southwick by the sea
And it was in my sleep one night
This story came to me
I fish from Southwick harbour arm
Right where he sailed, they say.
So this is yet another tale
Of one that got away!

2018

HARRISON

Thomas Harrison was one of the most fanatical anti-Royalists and a fearsome Civil War soldier.

Harrison was a lawyer, a friend of Cromwell he
In wartime a commander in the New Model Army
He rose to major general and bravely led the line
Brought Charles to London prisoner in 1649

This song's for Thomas Harrison, a bold and steadfast man
A rebel to the bitter end and staunch republican
His gruesome fate our history had never seen before -
Hung drawn and quartered by a foe he'd thrashed in war

He signed the king's death warrant, seventeenth of fifty-one
And when the second Charles returned another war he won
He led his men at Worcester where Parliament held sway
Then chased the king to Shoreham from where he skulked away

This song's for Thomas Harrison, a bold and steadfast man
A rebel to the bitter end and staunch republican
His gruesome fate our history had never seen before -
Hung drawn and quartered by a foe he'd thrashed in war

Cromwell made Lord Protector, Harrison made a stand
Four times condemned to prison at his old friend's command
He sided with the Levellers against the Grandees' might
Said, 'If not for equality, why did the Army fight?'

This song's for Thomas Harrison, a bold and steadfast man
A rebel to the bitter end and staunch republican
His gruesome fate our history had never seen before -
Hung drawn and quartered by a foe he'd thrashed in war

Attila The Stockbroker

When Monck the traitor brought the king back, Harrison did not flee
Arraigned as regicide he said 'You mostly did as me -
It was the will of Parliament.' Condemned to hang and bleed
He punched the executioner who carried out the deed

This song's for Thomas Harrison, a bold and steadfast man
A rebel to the bitter end and staunch republican
His gruesome fate our history had never seen before -
Hung drawn and quartered by a foe he'd thrashed in war

THE MAN WITH THE BEARD

A move from 1649 into 2018, lyrically if not musically, though there are many parallels in our 'distressed and divided Nation' today. This 'ancient & modern' cautionary tale about the dangers of a Jeremy Corbyn personality cult references the most famous JC of all, and 'Freeborn' John Lilburne, leader of the Levellers.

When the Man with the Beard he first appeared
The man they call JC
The scribes and Pharisees they all sneered
At the man they call JC
Like Lilburne he a vision saw
Of a world where none were working poor
And he vowed to make that vision law
The man they call JC

He cares for the young and the sick and the old
The man they call JC
And people are worth much more than gold
To the man they call JC
He stands up tall and he speaks the truth
And he mobilized the nation's youth
Got 40% in the voting booth
Did the man they call JC

But it's not one man, it's ideas that count
With the man they call JC
And we don't need a sermon on the mount
From the man they call JC
He's got Momentum, that's for sure
Like the New Model Army in days of yore
And we'll take from the rich and we'll give to the poor
With the man they call JC

So let's not build a personality cult
Round the man they call JC
Or another religion could be the result
With a man they call JC
He's not the Messiah or a naughty boy
But a man Murdoch wants to destroy
That's how we know he's the real McCoy
The man they call JC

PRINCE HARRY'S KNOB
A modern day Ragged Trousered Philanthropist's anthem.

Give Hester and Diamond their bonus
They deserve it, they do a good job
I want workhouses for the dole scroungers
And a picture of Prince Harry's knob
I work for my gaffer for nothing
I'm grateful he gives me a job
I'd swap all your bloody trade unions
For a picture of Prince Harry's knob

His knob, his knob, a picture of Prince Harry's knob, HIS KNOB!
His knob, his knob, a picture of Prince Harry's knob!

The country it just can't afford it
Those strikers they're all rent-a-mob
They should all doff their caps and be happy
With a picture of Prince Harry's knob
Don't give me your bleeding heart lecture
You middle class Guardian snob
Cos some of us live in the real world
With a picture of Prince Harry's knob

His knob, his knob, a picture of Prince Harry's knob, HIS KNOB!
His knob, his knob, a picture of Prince Harry's knob!

You Lefties and loonies and liberals
You should all shut your bloody gob
Cos all the likes of me ask for
Is a picture of Prince Harry's knob
I'm penniless, hapless and hopeless
And the state of my health makes me sob
But I'll work like a slave for my betters
With my picture of Prince Harry's knob

His knob, his knob, a picture of Prince Harry's knob, HIS KNOB!
His knob, his knob, a picture of Prince Harry's knob!
His knob, his knob, a picture of Prince Harry's knob, HIS KNOB!
His knob, his knob, a picture of Prince Harry's knob!

Yes I'll read the Sun and I'll believe it
With my picture of Prince Harry's knob

MY POETIC LICENCE

I hope you have enjoyed the first 40 years of Attila the Stockbroker.
To finish, a poem which I started my set with for many years, the title of one of my books...

Yo! I'm the MC of ranting rebel poetry!
I know my history and my identity
I'm independent, a red cottage industry
DIY from here to eternity...
Now let me tell you what's been going on:
I take inspiration from centuries long gone
Oral tradition of sedition, that's my position -
No court jester with a tame disposition!
Poetic licence? 40 years I've had one
And they don't come easy, they're not handed out for fun
You have to earn it, work and sweat and move -
Not get stuck in a dead poet bore groove.
I earned mine in dirty scummy punk clubs
Rock gigs, arts centres, festivals and dodgy pubs
And yes, once or twice I've had to fight -
But when a fascist hits a poet, the poet's doing something right!
I love words and I love 'em in the red and raw
I like to use them in ways they've not been used before
Want you to laugh and want you to think as well -
Bollocks to TV - this is live, as live as hell!
Oral tradition - the real origins of poetry.
Attila the Stockbroker - ranting rebel MC.
Dean of the Social Surrealist University.
Welcome to my wild poetic journey!

2006, updated 2020

Heart On My Sleeve

Plague mask and cycling helmet, Shoreham Lighthouse, August 2020

We're always interested to hear from readers, authors and fans. For contact, submissions, mail order and further information, please email books@cherryred.co.uk

Other titles available from Cherry Red Books:

A Godawful Small Affair
J.B. Morrison

A Plugged In State Of Mind:
The History of Electronic Music
Dave Henderson

All The Young Dudes:
Mott The Hoople & Ian Hunter
Campbell Devine

Best Seat In The House:
A Cock Sparrer Story
Steve Bruce

Bittersweet: The Clifford T Ward Story
David Cartwright

Block Buster! - The True Story of The Sweet
Dave Thompson

Burning Britain: A History Of UK Punk 1980 To 1984
Ian Glasper

Celebration Day: A Led Zeppelin Encyclopedia
Malcolm Dome and Jerry Ewing

Children of the Revolution:
The Glam Rock Encyclopedia
Dave Thompson

Crossover The Edge - Where Hardcore, Punk And Metal Collide
Alexandros Anesiadis

Death To Trad Rock: The Post-Punk fanzine scene 1982-87
John Robb

Deathrow: The Chronicles Of Psychobilly
Alan Wilson

Embryo:- A Pink Floyd Chronology 1966-1971
Nick Hodges And Ian Priston

Fucked By Rock
(Revised and Expanded)
Mark Manning (aka Zodiac Mindwarp)

Goodnight Jim Bob:On The Road With Carter USM
Jim Bob

Good Times Bad Times –
The Rolling Stones 1960-69
Terry Rawlings and Keith Badman

Hells Bent On Rockin:
A History Of Psychobilly
Craig Brackenbridge

Independence Days - The Story Of UK Independent Record Labels
Alex Ogg

Indie Hits 1980 – 1989
Barry Lazell

Irish Folk, Trad And Blues:
A Secret History
Colin Harper and Trevor Hodgett

Johnny Thunders: In Cold Blood
Nina Antonia

Kiss Me Neck –
A Lee 'Scratch' Perry Discography
Jeremy Collingwood

Music To Die For: The International Guide To Goth, Goth Metal, Horror Punk, Psychobilly Etc
Mick Mercer

***Never Known Questions –
Five Decades Of The Residents***
Ian Shirley

No More Heroes: A Complete History Of UK Punk From 1976-1980
Alex Ogg

***Number One Songs In Heaven -
The Sparks Story***
Dave Thompson

Our Music Is Red - With Purple Flashes: The Story Of The Creation
Sean Egan

Prophets and Sages: The 101 Greatest Progressive Rock Albums
Mark Powell

PWL: From The Factory Floor (Expanded Edition)
Phil Harding

Quite Naturally - The Small Faces
Keith Badman and Terry Rawlings

Random Precision - Recording The Music Of Syd Barrett 1965-1974
David Parker

Rockdetector: A To Zs of '80s Rock / Black Metal / Death Metal / Doom, Gothic & Stoner Metal / Power Metal and Thrash Metal
Garry Sharpe-Young

***Rockdetector: Black Sabbath –
Never Say Die***
Garry Sharpe-Young

Rockdetector: Ozzy Osbourne
Garry Sharpe-Young

Tamla Motown - The Stories Behind The Singles
Terry Wilson

The Day The Country Died: A History Of Anarcho Punk 1980 To 1984
Ian Glasper

***The Legendary Joe Meek -
The Telstar Man***
John Repsch

The Motorhead Collector's Guide
Mick Stevenson

The Rolling Stones' Complete Recording Sessions 1962-2002
Martin Elliott

The Secret Life Of A Teenage Punk Rocker: The Andy Blade Chronicles
Andy Blade

Those Were The Days - The Beatles' Apple Organization
Stefan Grenados

***Trapped In A Scene:
UK Hardcore 1985-89***

Ian Glasper

Truth... Rod Steward, Ron Wood And The Jeff Beck Group
Dave Thompson

Turn Up The Strobe - The History Of The KLF
Ian Shirley

You're Wondering Now – The Specials from Conception to Reunion
Paul Williams

CHERRY RED BOOKS

Please visit
www.cherryredbooks.co.uk
for further info and mail order

Also available from Cherry Red Books...

CHERRY RED BOOKS

ARGUMENTS YARD - ATTILA THE STOCKBROKER

A happy childhood ripped apart by his father's death and a ghastly scholarship. Early punk days rehearsing and playing in a Brighton burial vault, skeletons and all. How he got his stage name. His first play on John Peel. Battling Nazis at 1980s gigs. Miners' Strike, Wapping, Red Wedge. Six tours of East Germany, four before the Wall came down, and the very first illegal punk gig in Stalinist Albania. Filling in for Donny Osmond at the Marquee. And a billion other things. This is Attila's autobiography.

You couldn't make it up.

'My number one choice of book to read in 2016'

HUFFINGTON POST

ORDER NOW FROM CHERRY RED BOOKS

www.cherryred.co.uk/format/books